Kobe Bryan

The Inspiring Story Of The Greatest Laker Ever

Table of Contents

Introduction

Death in any case in unacceptable by us and if it is of someone we truly followed and feel strong about, and if it comes at an age like 41, you cannot help but wonder what if this grave day never came to this earth! What if we still had the NBA legend with us doing his magic in the creative industry, in the sports industry, in helping the society and building up new athletes! It is still difficult for people to accept that the soon to be Hall of Famer Kobe Bryant is no longer there and had an accidental death at the age of 41. Not only his fans but also his retractors were shocked at this sudden departure of the NBA legend. You do not have to be his fan to appreciate what he achieved in his accidentally cut short life. In his 20 years long career, Kobe faced much love from the Lakers teammates, the NBA national team and the country. His popularity was present in China too and anywhere around the world where people were fans of basketball in general.

Kobe's reputation did not stay limited in the NBA alone; he was a great father of four and a very good businessman and a donator. He was a devoted husband and loved his wife very much and the entire world applauded their long cherished marriage. He had only one hurdle in the marriage back in 2003 but it was sorted out gracefully by Kobe and Vanessa. Since 2003, their relationships grew even stronger and they became idol like for many other couples for sustaining the marriage for so long.

Kobe's vision was always to leave a mark on people's heart as a good human being. Not only as an NBA legend because he wanted to bring a change in people's mind. His investments prove his target was to improve the condition of the society and working with anyone and everyone with little potential. He had a neat eye to see into people's innate self and bring out the confidence in people to dream big and chase after their dreams. He basically wanted to make anyone who loves sports dream big and chase for it with all their passion and his foundation backed up their passion with proper training and fundings.

In his 20 years of NBA career, he stood strong with the Lakers, the very first team he ever joined as a professional NBA player. He had many opportunities to switch and get paid more, but he decided not to change his first NBA team due to emotional attachments. His image of a 17-year-old teenager coming right into the NBA still gives goose-bumps to many. His early childhood was spent in Italy since his father played there professionally. So Kobe was always a little shy adjusting to the US lifestyle and anyone would be coy at that age.

In 2007-08 Season, Kobe was the most valuable player in the NBA as he won five NBA titles and two MVP awards. On top of that, he became the all-time leading scorer for the 4th time in his NBA career. Kobe was always one of the top picks for the NBA National Team, NBA All-Star team, and the Olympics. His skills and dedication made him an unforgettable player that even the detractors agree that he was unique in the basketball court and should be idolized as a great NBA player.

Kobe was very young when he got exposed to stardom and it had both ups and downs. Mostly positives though! Kobe and Shaquille O'Neal had a very good duo in their Lakers matches but occasionally they had some differences. After O'Neal switched teams, Kobe and O'Neal sorted out their differences and they became sociable with each other and many media news noticed it.

Kobe's partnership with his friend Jeff Stibel was very strong too and their strong bond led them to co-founding their foundation which made successful investments and made a lot of profit both inside and outside the sports industry.

Kobe always thought about the unfortunate people and you could see its proof in his investments. He did not care about someone's ethnicity or age or creed, he only believed in someone's passion and uplifting that passion into something broad. Kobe did not have a heart of gold, he also had a mind that could calculate things very well.

Kobe was a solid brand builder and every brand wanted to work with him. Any new entrepreneur would try to book an appointment with Kobe because in the sports industry if Kobe approved of someone or some product, suddenly that person becomes famous and hit overnight. Kobe's this ability led their foundation to make many successful investments and they made many entrepreneurs start their gig without much struggles.

Kobe had big dreams for the sports industry and he wanted to help out the youth and underprivileged kids. This shows how kind hearted Kobe was and how giving he was by nature. He could have lived a life of luxury, sit back relaxed at home or going on vacation with his wife and kids after his retirements from NBA, but he choose to invest his time with care and to make a change in the society. Most people with his net worth would be sitting at home, playing virtual games, or going on world tours to invade the world where Kobe was always busy trying out new creative ways to increase the quality of sports in his country and in China for the underprivileged kids. He also splurged into the film industry to tell creative sports stories to inspire millions. The stories he wanted to tell had a lot to do with his own life, his own struggles and his achievements and his life learnt lessons. Whenever someone pours their own stories, his struggles into art, it becomes very relatable and so were his film and his book. Both did very well and it made a significant mark on people's heart.

Kobe always dreamt big and always encouraged people to dream big, but he could not fulfill all of his dreams but we can hope his friends and family would continue the legacy that Kobe left behind.

Who Is Kobe Bryant?

He is the vibrant soul who has trampled on the basketball court for 20 years. He is the force to thrill the NBA followers with his performance. He is one of the remarkable players of the 21st century who redefined the arts of basketball playing and put it at the highest peak in our mind. He is a magician who cast a spell on us and we cannot break through the snare after his retirement, even after his death. Kobe Bryant lived his life filled with achievements and he kept dreaming big in every point of his life. First it was for the NBA, then for Music, then it went to doing charity and finally after his retirement we say this NBA athlete telling stories in screen. No adjective is enough to describe his excellence. He is an adjective for himself.

Bryant was one of the most famous and valued professional basketball players in America of his time. He entered the American National Basketball Association (NBA) right out of the high school as the shooting guard and passed twenty seasons of his professional career in the same league with the Lakers of Los Angeles. All through his basketball career, his outstanding performances brought him a lot of achievements.

The accolades he owns are All-NBA member team for 15 times, All-star for 18 times, the All-Defensive Team member for 12 times, twice NBA Finals Most valuable Player (MVP) winner, and NBA MVP in 2008. All of these achievements are not just mere numbers, but years of training, various scarifies on Kobe's end brought this track record which seems very fascinating when you look at Kobe's NBA career graph!

For two seasons he made the highest score in the NBA and it was a milestone for Kobe and his supporters and despite all those rumors and injuries he had to go through, he snatched those titles effortlessly. He has also acquired fourth place both in the All-time regular league for the regular season as well as for the past season. All these achievements of his professional life have made him one of the greatest basketball players of all time.

Since his childhood, he was very passionate about basketball as he was exposed to this game at a young age due to his father's profession. Throughout his growing up there was only sleeping, eating, and dreaming about playing basketball as growing up all he saw was this game. He cannot remember a single day that he has passed without hearing the bounce of the basketball. From his early years, when other children pass their Sundays watching cartoons, he never felt any love for these time pass elements. He used to practice with the basketball and he kept hearing a whisper from the basketball court that he could not refused.

As an enthusiastic player, he decided his future at a very young age. An Italian Journalist Andrea Barocci, who published "An Italian Name Kobe", said, "It became very clear very early on that, that he knew he was the best". He always nourished the dream of playing as the professional player of the NBA. Passions, determination, enthusiasm, and practice in him have worked to give America a very talented player. His dream was big, he loved the game but the inspiration also came from his father and mother.

Kobe was from a royal basketball family as both his father and mother's side he inherited the quality of this game. His father was a former professional basketball player, Joe Bryant and his mother is Pamela Cox Bryant. Both Kobe's parents played the game and it had significant impact on Kobe as a young child. You cannot really compare an average kid's childhood with Kobe's as he was exposed to many things that directly connected him with basketball. These connections, these influences, the passion of his parents slowly but surely transported to him without any grand announcement.

Joe Bryant, or Jellybean by the nickname, was a Professional basketball player in America and is currently working as the coach. After passing three successful years in the La Salle University, he was selected by the Golden State Warriors in the year 1975 in the first round. But in the meantime, of starting the Golden State season, one of his homeland team, Philadelphia 76ers, makes deal with him and Joe remained in the team for four seasons. After that, he played for the San Diego Clippers for three years from 1979 to 1982. With the finishing of the NBA final season, Joe moved for Europe for a better career and better opportunity in the continent of culture. These constant switches is only to have a better life and a better basketball career, it was nothing personal, Joe never had any problems with any of his teammates.

He shifted to Northern Italy and played for Italian A1 League and Italian A2 League clubs for seven seasons. There he joined the AMG Sebastiani Rieti at first in 1984 and continued to 1986, then passed one year with the Viola Reggio Calabria team, and then finished his Italian career with Reggio Emilia in 1991. Italy has seen a lot of changes in the fate of Joe.

At last, he reaches the pro ranks. With a chance to use all his skills and talents he acquired throughout his growing up in Philadelphia, over-poured the success tank, and became a star. In every game, his point used to remain 30 to 40. So, both his salary and respect and endorsement increased at that point. This is what Joe strived after from one country to a complete new culture and it was really a great time for the Bryant family and from then they never looked back. During his years with Reggio Emilia, he owned the Player of the Year award twice which is also reassuring for him that he was doing well in Italy.

Then finishing his glorious Italian part Joe returned to America and continued playing even in his fifties for the American Basketball Association. This shows the brick solid ambition of Joe that seems to find his place even at such age! After completing his playing career, he has started working as the coach and continues working at the same post still today. The amount of experience, the struggles, the switches and the training he went through, he can now teach it to others, which can only be a good thing for any player to get first hand training from such a versatile player.

Joe's professional career is like a fast and adventurous journey but his family life is something everyone always wondered and complimented about. Joe and Pam are complements to each other as they still the example of a happy conjugal relationship. Joe had a crash for Pam since his childhood and they never got tired of each other. The grandparents of both lived in Philadelphia, in the same block and they had passed each other on the street many times in the 1960s. It was a sweet love story that built by itself naturally over the years. They had the chance to revive their childhood crush in the college days at the beginning of the 1970s and decided to get married soon.

Throughout their married life Pam has always supported and encouraged Joe at every step. It was not a easy task to leave a country where you grew up with your family behind to support your husband. She did not care and she was not afraid to go into a new culture and a new way of life. This shows what a sacrificing mind she cultured and such a lovely relationship could only bring up a glorious star like Kobe. The life of his father and mother was open to him to learn. His father was the lively hero to teach every step of basketball. He got the chance to watch the basketball games of his father closely. So, he got the chance to get a lesson of playing from close contact and to include the tricks in his own practice. The prosperous family, as well as the carrier life of Bryant, is actually the reflection of the early teachings of his parents.

As he grew up, during his teenage days he met the love of his life, Vanessa Bryant. They met each other on the spot of a music video shooting in 1999. Vanessa was a high school senior and Kobe was only 20. It may seem like an unconventional bond to begin with and for many it seemed like a fling that would end in months or perhaps in years but Kobe and Vanessa was not fooling around with each other. They had marriage in mind and they felt very strongly about each other.

They tied the marital knot in 2001 and it came as a shock to Kobe's parents and the fans were also surprised that this soon to be star made such a drastic move so early in his life. Although the fans made peace with it later and was happy that Kobe is happy in a conjugal relationship. From then, through all of his ups and downs, Vanessa remained beside him. The teens have grown up together and are the best friends throughout the life journey. The relationship between them was so strong that no storm could break it down. This is the power that has given Bryant the strength to continue his successful career in the basketball field in the latter part of his life. She always encouraged him, and he also supported her in doing what pleased her.

Apart from being a good NBA player, a good business man, Kobe was really a family man. Kobe became a great father and always tried to bond with them despite his busy schedule. He and his wife have given born to four children. As a father, he was always responsible and caring for his children despite the hectic lifestyle he had to endorse. He regularly posted his family photos on his Instagram account which shows he is a family man and enjoys sharing their activities with the world. His daughters were his princesses like any other daughter to their fathers. Once he said in an interview that he actually becomes a teddy bear when he remains at home with his lovely children. Like his father, Joe, Kobe has tried hard to guide his daughters himself. He encouraged them to build up the love for different types of sports like basketball, volleyball, and soccer.

He became the coach to Gigi who in her early days became a renowned basketball player. She always got Kobe by her side as the mentor because out of all the kids, Gigi was the one who built the love for basketball more extensively than the others. Due to Gigi's love for basketball, some says maybe it was destined that he and Gigi shall take their last breath together.

Early Childhood

It was a happy family of Joe Bryant and Pam with their two daughters. Joe was playing as the forward player of the team Philadelphia 76ers. They were eager for a boy after two lovely daughters and God listened to them. They were gifted with a lovely Heaven made child who can make their life glorious one day. So, Kobe Bryant was born at Lankenau Hospital in Montgomery County and boy! It was a remarkable day for the Bryant couple to welcome their third child and the only son of the family.

Sharia Bryant and Shaya Bryant are the elder sisters of Kobe and they were gleeful to have a brother among them. As the elder siblings, they were always affectionate to him and Kobe felt respect and appreciation very much from his sisters all through his life. He used to praise them to be very talented and college-educated scholars. Their lovely relationship has a great beginning with acute childhood and dependency on each other.

As the Bryant couple was excited about their son, they fixed their son's name beforehand. There is a story behind the name 'Kobe' and you may have heard this name at any Japanese restaurants before. Yes, this name belongs to a very special Japanese dish and once the Bryant couple heard the name, they immediately decided their son should be named after a Japanese dish! This sounds rather outrageous but you have hear the whole story to find sense in it!

Pam and Joe went to a Japanese restaurant one time and while looking at the menu card and their eyes stopped at world-famous Kobe beef. They immediately rhymed it with Jellybean, which was Joe's nickname and they could not see a better name for their son than Kobe Bean! Kobe made a name for himself in the history of NBA and despite the unusual name picking story behind his name, it got engraved in people's heart for the things he did as a human being.

Joe always wanted to make Kobe a basketball player and with this view in mind, he started inserting love for basketball from his very childhood. Kobe's life then revolved every day with his father's basketball schedule. Very often Joe took him to his afternoon practices and tried to make Kobe interested in it. He used to take Kobe with him always whenever he started for any tournament. Kobe never missed any game of his father as he always loved the kick and the excitements that lie with every game. He used to read the moves of his father carefully and to reflect them in his playing.

During the halftime of the play, he entertained the audience by shooting the baskets. Joe took him to the gym regularly and he often climbed the hoops during his father's play. So his father's friends had to keep an eye on him even when they are playing. As someone fell on the ground, he came with a mope on the court to clean up everything.

Kobe's interest in being an NBA star became acute as his grandfather recorded and sent him the video clips in Italy in those days before the starting of the International Cable Sport feeds of different basketball events every week. Joe would sit beside his son to watch the videos and the one which Joe got during his scouting days in America, and to teach his son different tricks of playing basketball. With these videos Kobe got the scope to watch the court at a full and the way of unfolding the acting during a play. Joe also put a basketball ring in the garden for Kobe's regular practice. Kobe got the golden chance to get a father like Joe for his future success.

Kobe was fond of playing basketball and football and he also watched most of the games in TV. In his childhood days, he was a diehard supporter of basketball team 'Los Angeles Lakers' and the 'AC Milan' basketball team. But there were some instincts which provoked him to say that one day he would be a basketball star by his third birthday. And his prediction was correct as we all know now. Not only his father but the people who were the witness of his growing up could also anticipate the future in him.

When he was only six, his father shifted from the USA to an ancient European country in 1984. Joe joined the country basketball team there in Rieti and this transition had a great impact on the children of the Bryant family. Especially, on Kobe, to get introduced to a country of an ancient civilization since he was born in US. Rieti is a small, calm medieval city at the center of Italy which had only 40,000 residents. So, a difference was evident for small Kobe of the peaceful place with his crowded Philadelphia which was now far away from him. There was the local basketball team, AMG Sebastiani, not any NBA or 76ers.

The Bryant family was on a move throughout their stay and they changed the places with the changing of a team of Joe. Every place brought a new experience to Kobe, at first, they were in Rieti, later they moved to Reggio Calabria, then Pistoia, and finally moved to Reggio Emilia. The last place had advantages for both Joe and the family, as Kobe first realized his love for basketball and joined the junior team for the first time in his life. He expressed his love for Reggio Emilia as he visited later years.

All of his good feelings, bad feelings, passions, and emotions build up in Italy. His childhood spent breathing the scent of Italy and to him, his homeland was not America rather Italy.

When Kobe first came to Italy he was full of energy and his Odyssey of the basketball continued. The landscape and language of common people there were unknown to them and they did not know any locals either. They had nowhere to go and none to talk with which also led Kobe and his sisters to create a special bond between each other.

They had to be dependent on each other and every day, as they came back from school they used to practice the new Italian words and tried to converse among them. With this practice, they could be perfectly fluent in the Italian language within a few months. This also helped bridging the gap between the siblings.

On the off days of Joe, the whole family mostly enjoyed the sightseeing adventurous tours together. The time was a very lovely moment for the Bryant family and anyone who witnessed them could see how happy they were. If there was no tour, the family visited the families of the American players. Among Joe's American friend was Harvey Catchings, former NBA star who moved to Italy for one year to join the Italian basketball team. His two daughters Tamika and Tauja were the future stars in their college and also in the WNBA. The Bryant and Catchings' family together visited the Roman ruins and from this place, Kobe and his sisters could learn the broader perspective of life and learnt to dream big in life.

Thus, life was of fun, entertainment, and enjoyment. Such is the way Kobe views his father's famous life where there was nothing to worry about. Joe's lifestyle of being crowded by the fans all the time was inspiring to Kobe and he always saw the positivity of the NBA lifestyle. Kobe always fascinated about being a NBA star seeing his father's lifestyle and how people accepted him. Italy had another sport that was in the limelight, soccer! The soccer-crazy people of Europe tried to lead Kobe in another direction. Many times they told him that with his leaping capability, fast movability, and long hands he would become perfect goal-keeper. Kobe also had some interest in soccer but with time he became more serious with his basketball career and that was the right decision he took.

The Italian sports journalist Andrea Barocci said whenever talking about Kobe's childhood, "Aged 6, Kobe would often jump off the balcony of his parents' house, cross a busy road. Going to the church playground and practicing basketball was a hobby for him. He also added saying that Kobe knew from his childhood that he was the best. This belief got deep-rooted in his mind from then and he made other people understand this even as he was a boy.

As he started playing football for the junior team he became a friend to other players who still remember him proudly. Among them, Davide Giudici, junior teammate, and a long-term friend said, Kobe always dreamt of joining the NBA. Because of this dream many people poke fun at Kobe. But they knew that he was a very hard-working boy. Where the other boys would enjoy the TV or remain busy doing other things, he continued his practice in their garden.

His determination and commitment to basketball could only bring him the achievements he owes. His former coach of Reggio Emilia Andrea Menozzi said, "He was very determined. From what I gather, he never lost that attitude." Thus both senior and junior Bryant became famous among their neighbors and they still remember Kobe as their own.

Bryant played in the youth group when he was a child. But sometimes he competed with the full-aged man from his father's group. Brian Shaw, who played against his father said, "I knew him from playing against his father when he was 9 or 10 years old, and then I had the opportunity to play against him, to play with him, to win championships, and also coach him for a couple of years," His enthusiastic mind never let him say no. He had a fire within him and its ray has always strengthened him to be successful. Even, when he was in his grade school he used to always compete with his father one-on-one. And Joe was happy to share, "He used to always beat me one-on-one, but would forget the score. Whenever he asked, I always told him I was up by two." He was so much confident of his skill that he got never afraid before anyone. He was always ready to move forward.

During the Summer-time, Kobe with his family went to Philadelphia to pay a visit to his grandparents. With this he got a scope to compete with the American children in court. But at first, things were not in his favor. He did not make a point throughout the whole summer season. We're going to love you if you score zero or 50." So, he never felt disappointed and try for the best he could give throughout his life.

Italy was his adopted home and he always paid tribute to this country for his rearing. None can ever think that such an NBA star could grow up in the countries of Italy but his life has given him a lesson that everything is possible. One of his childhood friends, Alessia Pierattini whom he paid a visit seven years before his death, said that Kobe wanted to bring his daughters in Italy to live.

Kobe had to leave Italy at the age of 13 and go back to Philadelphia, unable to use even the English slangs. By this time he became a perfect Italian with his language, attitudes, gestures, and an Italian mind. He never could detach himself from Italy and he felt such a love for Italy that he had to come back again and again to recall his childhood memories.

High School Career

Kobe was different from his friends and classmates in high school and anyone who met him could sense a spark in him that was easy to notice. He went to Ardmore, Philadelphia at Lower Merion High School. In decades there was no other freshman who could enter into the Merion's varsity's team. Kobe was special and the varsity team recognized his skills and decided to offer him a spot in the team. In the beginning, the team did not do so well and had a score of 4-20 record but with constant training and with firm focus, they began to improve their skills gradually. For the next three years, they scored pretty high with 77-13 record and Kobe played in all the five positions because he was equally good in all the positions.

He averaged 311 points, 5.2 assists and 10.4 rebounds in his junior year. The score was impressive and it gave him the title of Pennsylvania Player of the Year. College recruiters noticed Kobe's skills and performances and Kobe's goal was also to impress the on-lookers. Kobe preferred Duke, North Carolina, Villanova, and Michigan but after 1995 Kobe decided to go directly to the pros.

Kobe's high school career was as impressive as his NBA career. He with his techniques and basketball skills became an all-time best scorer in southeastern Pennsylvania basketball as his assisting the Lower Merion Aces made 31-3 record. He also led the team to Class-AAAA state championship. Kobe started leading the team at a very young age in his life and this trait of leading continued even in his NBA career. He was so successful at it that this opportunity came one after another to him.

NBA Draft until Final Season (Include championship runs)

Kobe's First Contract

Kobe was at a very early age recognized to be one of the best basketball players in the country. Due to his father's influence on him, he grew a passion for this game quite naturally. His passion got flared with the help of his school, the sports counselors and the appreciation he got at an early age. After graduation, he was selected by Charlotte Hornets for the 1996 NBA draft and for Kobe it was a dream came true. He went on cloud 9 as he always dreamt of this day, but he never thought this event come in his life so soon. Just imagine one thing that you dreamt of achieving all your life, and you wish to grab it at a certain age but with God's decree, it clings on to you much earlier than expected, how would you feel? Exactly, you will be speechless and in awe, so was the reaction of Kobe when he got into NBA team officially!

He was the 13th draft pick in the team but just a day before the final draft they decided to trade Kobe with Vlade Divac. The Lakers' were also looking for someone who can free up the salary cap and throw the ball to the free-agent center. The Lakers asked the Hornets who will the Lakers' like to trade. It was a rather last-minute decision as Kobe was the only person who was a first guard drafted from the high school straight. For Kobe, it did not matter that he was being traded, for him the fact that he is joining the NBA is what mattered the most. Deep down inside, he only wanted to play and prove to people his potentiality in the basketball court.

Vlade Divac was rather resistant about the trade and he even wanted to retire as opposed to being traded from Los Angeles. He thought it would be wiser to retire than being traded with Kobe Bryant as it did somewhat upset him. His reaction not outrageous, in fact, anyone in his position would feel somewhat devastated. It was on June 30th when Divac tamed down and made peace with the decision of trading. The final trade took place on July 9, 1996 and it was the time when the offseason moratorium ended.

Kobe was still 17 at that moment so he could not sign his papers at that time. Kobe's parent cosigned the contract until he turned 18 and the season began right after he turned 18. His first contract was for $3.5 Million as a rookie for three years. As a teenager, this number did not bother him and he was happy about joining the NBA than about the money. At such young age, people are more eager to prove themselves amongst the world than to earn big bucks.

Adjusting To The NBA Life

Kobe's first-ever match was in California for the Summer Pro League which was in Long Beach. His debuted match was something his parents and his schoolmates were looking forward to. He did not disappoint his family or the coach or others. He scored 25 points in his very first match and it did impress everyone watching him. As a debut game he played significantly good and there was not a single ounce of nervousness in him for playing with professional NBA players.

Kobe's first ever NBA game was in a standing room only crowd and they cheered to encourage the teams. Lakers' coach Del Harris was very impressed with Kobe and he did not see many people to play that good in their debut games. Kobe was only debuting in this match but still the defenders were struggling hard to come in front of Kobe. The impeccable performance also impressed the West. In the finale, he managed to score 36 points and his average was about 24.5 points in four games with 5.3 rebounds in those four games. For a debutant in a basketball game, this score is significantly impressive and people began to grow immediate interest in Kobe.

Although he was only a rookie he was still turning heads which is not unusual at all. People were very interested in his playing and they would look up to what Kobe would do next. His was young, he had a different style of his own and he owned his versatility without any doubt. He was popular as a high-flyer in the basketball ground.

He was only 18 when he was doing his magic as a rookie in 1996-1997 games and he used to guard Nick Van and Eddie Jones at that time. He was the youngest NBA player then and before his joining the NBA, Jermaine O'Neil and Andrew Bynum were the youngest NBA players. On top of that, Kobe became the youngest NBA player starter.

(18 years, 158 days). Kobe could break so many records due to joining the NBA so early and of course improving his skills with every game.

In the beginning, his playing time in the ground was fairly limited which is the case for most of the rookies. You have to prove to the world and especially to the coach before you get more limelight in the basketball court. But with his progress on the game, his time was increased gradually and he found around 15.5 minutes per game by the end of the season. It did not take him too long to be a fan favorite as he won the Slam Dunk Contest in 1997. It was only in his second season and he was awarded as an All-star. This news came to Kobe and his family as a complete surprise and boy, what a wonderful surprise it was! Being only 18, he won the title of youngest slam dunk champion in 1997. Kobe was unique and all the members along with his coach recognized it easily. He earned himself a spot at the NBA all-rookie second team and he shared this opportunity with his teammate Travis Knight.

Kobe's First-Ever Leading Moment In The Team

When Lakers had a playoff with Utah Jazz, Kobe found his first ever leading moment after joining the NBA. It was the semifinals of the Western Conference. Kobe got a leading role in game 5 and the first 4 games went pretty average manner. It was a very important match because most of the top-notch players were somehow out of the game. Robert Horry could not enter the game because of his fight with Utah's Jeff Hornacek and Byron Scott had his wrist sprained, so he could not make it to the game either. In the fourth quarter, Shaquille O'Neal fouled out with 1:46 and at the end of the game, Kobe shot four airballs. In the fourth quarter, Kobe missed a game-turning 2 point jump shot and at the very last minute, Kobe miss-fired two tying shots.

Everyone was very shocked by his playing and this shock was definitely a positive one. His fellow teammate O'Neal commented those bold shots could only be made by Kobe and no one else dared at that moment to shot like Kobe.

Kobe was always either to show what he had learnt in his teen years and constant practices but Kobe could show off his talent as a young guard only during his second season. His teammates and the coach could rely on him more by that time since he had more game time, his scores also doubled. His points got to 15.4 from 7.6 for each game and in 1998, the Lakers' pushed forward Kobe to play small forward with the guard in small games. For Kobe, it was a dilemma whether to accept this or refuse it because he always had bigger games in mind. For a good basketball player, dreaming big is the ultimate key to going up and improving to the best of their physical ability and Kobe always dreamt big.

The First Award

Kobe was declared the runner up for NBA's 6th Man of the Year Award which came to him as a big surprise and he almost pinched himself to see if this was real! He won the youngest NBA All-Star starter through fan voting and he had a good line of fans following him throughout the country. He made history with this win as no other man in NBA history won this title before. His teammates, Van Exel, O'Neal, and Jones were selected to play in the All-star game. It was also another history that four-man from the same team were nominated to play in the All-star game at the same time. Kobe's 15.4 points were unbeatable as no other player reached it in that season. Both Kobe's points and his popularity begin to reach high pecks and it only motivated him further to train harder for the game.

Kobe emerged as a premium guard during the 1998-99 Season and earlier Jones or Van Exel used to start the game but this was traded. Kobe began to start every game in Lockout Shortened Season and in this very season, he also signed an extension on his contract. They knew where Kobe's career was going and no one wanted Kobe to switch the team, so everyone made Kobe very comfortable in the team. The extension was for 70$ Million and it was for six years. For this contract, Kobe stayed with the Lakers till 2003-04.

He was far away from Michael Jordan and Magic Johnson both in terms of experience and age but still, people started comparing him to them. Kobe's skills were so impressive that sportswriters could not help but compare Kobe with the best players of NBA history. Unfortunately, all those praises did not translate into the game and in that Season the Lakers' lose the game with San Antonio Spurs. This lose did disappoint many people but Kobe's fan following did not decrease by even one number.

1999

Kobe found himself in a good spot when Phil Jackson took over the Lakers' as a coach in 1999. Kobe improved with every game and his coach had supported him along the journey of improving and sustaining his impeccable skills. His improvements earned him more time in the game and with more time in the game, the scope of scoring higher increased for Kobe.

With the reliability of the coaches and the teammates, Kobe became a premier shooting guard. He appeared in the League's All-NBA, All-Defensive and All-Star teams and all of these responsibilities never came as a burden for Kobe. He enjoyed the process and with every game the fans and the detractors could see him trying to be the best version of himself.

Kobe and O'Neal developed a legendary center guard duo which led them to contend for NBA championships. The coach Phil Jackson put up a strategy to win six championships and the strategy was to implement the triangle offense. Both the players followed it well and it helped Kobe and O'Neal gain the elite class in NBA society.

2000-2001

Kobe had a terrible hand injury due to which he had to refrain from playing in the 1999-2000 season. It was a very crucial time both for Kobe and the Lakers' but you cannot really help it when your body starts to give up on your dreams! This is how Kobe must have felt when his mind was 100% focused on the game but he could not translate that energy into the game due to the sudden injury. His injury occurred during the preseason game with Washington Wizards. After his hand got better and he came back, his energy was better than ever. He played about 38 minutes per game and his points also went up and so were his skills.

With the direction and guidance of the strategy master Phil Jackson, the Lakers' won three championships in a row. The Los Angeles Lakers' was fortunate to chase 2001-2002 NBA championship three times in a row. This also proves his plan of Kobe and O'Neal was a hit and the powerful partnership between Kobe and O'Neal was so effective that it gave them 67 wins. All these wins led Kobe to be awarded as the All-NBA Team

Second Team and not only that he was also tilted as the All-NBA Defensive Team. This was first in his career, so definitely the joy was immense for all his fans and teammates. The celebration got doubled because in the history of NBA, Kobe was the youngest to receive the title. O'Neal also got awarded the MVP because of his impeccable performance in that Season.

In 2000, a game against the Indiana Pacers, unfortunately, Kobe got an ankle injury and the timing could not have been worse! It happened to be the finals and it was a very important match for Kobe and his team. He landed on Jalen Rose's foot and hurt his ankle badly. It was during the 2nd quarter of game 2 and no matter how hard Kobe wanted to continue the game he could not due to the gravity of the injury. Rose did admit later the injury was evoked intentionally as Kobe was a big threat as an opponent. He put his foot under Kobe intentionally so his performance should be compromised.

Kobe had to rest and he skipped Game 2 and Game 3 but he could not sit back anymore and decided to come back in Game 4. In the second half of the game, Kobe could score 22 points, and despite the injury, Kobe still could lead his team to an OT victory. O'Neal fouled himself out of the game and Kobe with an ankle injury was the only hope left for Lakers'. Kobe did not disappoint to everyone's surprise and he scored the winning shot. The Lakers' won with 120-118 and with 6 games, the average score was 116-111. The last time the Lakers' won a Championship was back in 1988 and this was a memorable victory for the Lakers' since 1998.

Kobe played quite in the same manner in 2000-2001 Season too but the only thing that was new in this Season was he did advance with his points. He scored 28.5 points per game which was pretty good if you look at the NBA scoring graph.

In this Season the successful duo between Kobe and O'Neal began to crack as they could no longer co-exist in the same team without drawing unnecessary attention towards their dissimilarities. They had a very successful duo on the basketball grounds but outside the game they had dissimilarities and during 2000-01 Season the dissimilarities began to surface. Kobe did lead the game like previous seasons too but in this season the number of the win in comparison to the previous season decreased for the Lakers' as they had only 56 wins.

In the playoff, however, the Lakers' responded with 15-1 and the rivalry between the two leading teammates of the team did not come as a problem. First, they won over Portland Trail Blazers and this win was very easy. In the semifinals, they faced Sacramento Kings and the Lakers' successfully swept them away with Kobe scoring 48 points in his game 4. The winning score was 119-113 which was pretty impressive and they advanced to the finals. In the finals, they came head to head with Philadelphia 76ers and the Lakers' knew it will not be an easy win against this team.

The Lakers' lose the first game but they won the remaining four games. Kobe, of course, had his heavy moments in the game and he scored 29.4 points on an average. He had 7.3 rebounds with 6.1 assists points and this score not only impressed the fans and the crowd but also O'Neal. O'Neal could not help but praise Kobe publicly for the impeccable moves, skills and energy. Kobe was also included in the All-NBA Team Second Team and the All-NBA Defensive Team for the 2nd time and he had the opportunity to start the All-Star NBA game again. This fortune came for the third time in a row for him and although he was lucky to achieve all of these in one season but no one can deny his hard-work is responsible mainly to achieve all that.

2001-2002

2001-2002 Season was glorious for Kobe in terms of playing the most games in his entire NBA career. He managed to play 80 games in this Season and prior to this Season he never could bring in this much efficiency to the basketball court. He scored 56 points on January 14, 2002 and it was his highest score in his career. His rebound score was 5 and his assists points were 4 and they won with 120-81 glorious score against the Memphis Grizzlies. If you look at the final score, you can imagine what a match it must have been for the Lakers' to make the final score significant of 39 points difference.

His all-round play with 25.2 points per game continued and his rebounds were 5.5 rebounds and assists points were 5.5. Kobe's career-high shooting score was 46.9% and this high score also led Kobe to assist the Lakers' again. By this time, Kobe was used to assisting the team with highly efficient skills and most of the times it paid the team well.

A match against Philadelphia 76ers was very significant in Kobe's playing career. He made a bold or rather outrageous statement that they are, "going to cut their hearts out", referring to the 76ers. Kobe was very blunt in this comment but it made the onlookers very uncomfortable especially because this game took place in Philadelphia itself. So the audience was against the Lakers' mostly. The audience was very strong in their hatred towards Kobe during the entire game as he already angered the audience by stating that obnoxious statement before the game starts. All you could hear the crowd booing during the game and it did somehow triggered some anxiety amongst the Lakers'. But Kobe was unmoved with the crowd's booing and he kept to his clam and focused on the game. His determination earned him a score of 31 points in this game. Because of this high performance, he grabbed himself the All-Star MVP award. He this time made it to the All NBA first team and this was happening for the first in this career. Despite the loud booing in the arena, his performance was not compromised for a minute. He took the hate and translated it into a power play in the ground.

In that year, the Lakers had victory in 58 games and they came in the second position in the Pacific Division. They were beaten by their in-state rivals, Sacramento Kings which was very disappointing for the entire team. On March 1, 2002, they faced the Indiana Pacers and in the very first game, Kobe was suspended and everyone in the team knew from that moment, this game will be very long and painful. Kobe punched Indiana Pacers, Reggie Miller and immediately got suspended from the game. To everyone's surprise, The Lakers' won the match and the fact that they could win without a star player like Kobe was motivating for the entire team.

The Lakers' journey to the finals this year was comparatively difficult as opposed to last year as Kobe had injuries, suspensions etc. They had to do a lot to retain their place in the finals but they were determined to give their 100% in each game. In the first game, the Lakers did successfully defeat the Blazers but in the second game, they swept away the San Antonio Spurs with highly efficiency and great game-play. The Lakers' doubted the Sacramento Kings and the Lakers' home-court advantage was not there. The series had 7 games. After 2000, the Western Conference Finals, this happened for the first time with the Lakers and with many struggles, Lakers' again managed to win over their division rivals. The Lakers appeared for the third time in the NBA finals and this win arrived hope to win the championship one more time in their hearts.

The Lakers' played with the New Jersey Nets in the finals and luckily Kobe managed to get 26.8 points per game and his rebounds were 5.8 and his assists points were 5.3 and his shooting was 51.4%. Kobe alone scored a quarter of the team points and Guess what? Kobe won three NBA

Championships' in a row at the age of only 23 and this was also another NBA record. Throughout the finals, Kobe's performance was noticeable and he was praised for being a good team player. His accountability was appreciated by all and this mind-blowing performance earned him the title, "clutch player".

2002-2003

The very first game of the season was not as good as the Lakers have planned or hoped for and they got defeated by the visiting San Antonio Spurs with a score of 87-82. Kobe scored 27 points in that game and his rebound score was 10 and his assists were 5. This was not only disappointing starting of a season for the Lakers but for Kobe's performance graph too.

Later on November 1 Kobe and the Lakers got some good news as they won with the LA Clippers and their score was 108-93. This time Kobe had a triple-double score and his scores were 33 points with 15 rebounds and 12 assists points. It was like a ray of hope that came towards the Lakers' with these good scores.

Later in the next year, January 7, 2003, Kobe managed to get an NBA record and it was for three-pointers in a game. The game was against Seattle Super Sonics and Kobe made 12 points against them. This was a golden time in Kobe's career and he managed to get an average of 30 points in all the games of that series.

Later in February, Kobe averages 40.6 points which allowed him to make history in the NBA world and his average rebound was 6.9 and assist points were 5.9. These points were the top scores of Kobe in his entire career and he was beginning to see the result of all those hard-work and compromises on his diet. Again Kobe was voted for the All-Defensive first teams and in All NBA which came as another motivational lift up for him to work harder on his skills. Kobe also scored himself the third place in the MVP award.

The Lakers finished with a score of 50-32 in the regular seasons and they came face to face with San Antonio Spurs in Western Conference in the semifinals. This was a crucial time for the Lakers' and they played very poorly in the playoffs. It was somewhat contradictory situation for Kobe as he was individually doing so well in terms of getting votes, getting nominated for different awards and teams but as a team, the Lakers' could not achieve what they have hoped for!

They lost all six games and San Antonio Spurs became the NBA champions and certainly this was not a successful season for the Lakers or Kobe.

Next year, things started to lighten up for the Lakers' and they could snag themselves team members like Karl Melone and Gary Payton and both of them were NBA All-Stars. When you have All-Stars in the team, there is a mental strength you get to work harder and push yourself harder in the game. The Lakers' tried one more time for the NBA championship and there was good news at one end but bad news on another. The Lakers' acquired new NBA All-Star team members which was a ray of hope for the team but their star player Kobe was accused of sexual assault which dimmed the good news altogether.

Due to this unfortunate accusation, Kobe was often visiting the court and he had to miss various games due to attending court calls. Sometimes Kobe had a court call and a game on the same day and during that case, Kobe had to attend the call and then fly to attend the game. The sexual assault came right before the season would begin and it put Kobe and the team in a very difficult spot.

Although Kobe had missed many games in that season, fortunately, he could make it to the final game. In the final, the Lakers' faced Portland Trail Blazers and they could steal the victory from the Blazers but it was a very tough call. In the fourth quarter, Kobe scored a 3 pointer and it was a very difficult win but with firm focus they finally could steal it. The game had 1.1 seconds to send the game to overtime and the game did go to a second overtime. Kobe again shot a three-pointer and he also had to shot two buzzer-beaters. These two buzzer-beaters led the Lakers' to win the game.

Kobe's team had a good line up created by the coach and this time O'Neal started the game. Then Malone, Payton, and Kobe followed through and this line up worked for the

Lakers' quite efficiently. They did manage to get into the finals and they met with the Detroit Pistons. Detroit Pistons was not someone to overlook as they won their last championship back in the 1990s but still they were in good shape as a team.

The Lakers' initially thought they have the upper hand in this final game but they did not, however, get positive results. The very first five games were disappointing and the Lakers' lost again and the Detroit Piston won the NBA championship after a very long time. This lose again put the Lakers' in a really deep depression.

In this series, Kobe scored 22.6 points per game and assists score was 4.4 with shots 35.1%. Jackson as a coach did his best for the Lakers but it was time to renew his contract. Then Rudy Tomjanovich had the chance to coach the Lakers' and Rudy decided to make a trade as the Lakers' were starting to run a big losing track which was getting on everyone's nerves. He traded O'Neal for three different players and they were Brian Grant, Caron Butler, and Lamar Odom. The trade was done with the Miami Hearts and Rudy had a fully proven plan for the Lakers' with this important trade. O'Neal did perform some very good games and snatched many victories in the past but trading him with three other players was a strategic move for Lakers'. Kobe had an offer the very next day from the Los Angeles Clippers. Kobe did turn the offer down without much thought on it as he decided to stay with his first team. He signed a seven-year contract with the Lakers' again. This shows Kobe's dedication towards his team and how he wanted to improve the stat of the team with every game.

2004-2005

2003-2004 Season was also difficult for the Lakers' for sudden resign of their coach Rudy Tomjanovich and it had put the teammates into an anxious position. Rudy resigned due to his health issues but the Lakers' could not perceive what to do next! He resigned at the midway of the season so the remaining time of the season Lakers' was coached by Frank Hamblen and he was an assistant coach earlier.

Despite the resign of the coach, Kobe's performance did not decay by 1%, he kept on trying to get a good score for the team in all the games. He was then the 2nd top scorer with 27.6 points per game in the league. His performance was still good throughout the league but Basketball is a team game. His team was not enough to support Kobe's significant skills and in a team game, the supporting cast has to be as strong as your main team starter.

2004-2005 Season was somewhat difficult for Kobe as he had to cope with the personal accusation and his team's unfortunate loss in the previous seasons.

From one point he was battling to retain his reputation from that unusual sexual accusation and on another point, he was battling hard to win a game for the Lakers. His mental peace was damaged with the constant court calls, numerous lawsuits and the problems were tripled when Jackson wrote a book called, "The Last Season: A Team in Search of Its Soul".

People were already talking bad about Kobe's personal life and professional choices and the book made everything worst. The book focused on Lakers' fails in the 2003-2004 Season. The Lakers' performance for 2000, 2001, and 2002 was remarkable and they made many records and many histories for the NBA. When you compare those successes with their 2003-2004 failings, people generally could see the huge change in their fate or game-play. When you pit white against black, both the colors become very vibrant.

The book was like putting salt on the wounds for the Lakers'. When you are feeling low and down, you need the motivation to go forward. You do not need a mirror you reflect your failure and be told about all the wrong you have done. The book was doing exactly this for the Lakers.

In the book, Jackson had focused on Kobe more than other players in the team. Kobe had his glorious moments but his lows were more focused in the book. As if the Lakers are losing only because of Kobe's fault! Kobe was mentioned as "un-coachable" by Jackson in the book. This also ruined Kobe's impression of his personality as a player. This one word made Kobe seem arrogant and perhaps too proud of his past achievements to the world.

Kobe and the Lakers' missed their playoffs for the first time in 12 years. The Lakers score was 34-48. For the first time in Kobe's basketball playing history, he did not make it to the NBA All-Defensive team. He also got a demotion from All NBA First Team to the All NBA Third Team. Kobe's reputation further got damaged when he was having a public feud with Ray Allen and Malone. This public feud also happened in this very

Season. It seemed like every bad incident that could come into life came into life for Kobe.

2005-2006

Jackson did resign with the excuse that his health was not good, but deep down inside everyone knew it had something to do with his differences with Kobe. Despite all the differences, Jackson decided to come back to the Lakers and Kobe was the one who initiated this move. Kobe wanted Jackson back to coaching the Lakers' as this was needed for the team. People did wonder whether or not Kobe would be able to be in good relations with Jackson this time but for the betterment of the team, Kobe made peace with Jackson.

Kobe and Jackson successfully worked together for the Lakers' and their collaboration worked well and was apparent when the Lakers' made it to the playoffs again. In this Season, Kobe managed to break off all his previous scoring records. On December 20, 2005, the Lakers' faced with Dallas Mavericks and Kobe surprised everyone and scores 62 points in three quarters. When they went into the fourth quarter, Kobe single-handedly outscores the entire Dallas Team with 62-61. Since the intro of the shot clock, this happened only once by Kobe.

On January 16, 2006, the Lakers' faced with Miami Heart and everyone was eager to see this mage. Kobe and O'Neal had their problems and it was very public. Everyone knew about it but before the game, both of them shook their hands and hugged each other. This made headlines because people now knew both of them are becoming mature and moving on with professional life. Their feud was gone soon when the world saw Kobe and O'Neal were laughing and enjoying the 2006 NBA All-star game.

In January 2006, the Lakers' faced the Toronto Raptors and this was a sky-high moment for Kobe as he scored 81 points in the game. He never scored this high before in this career and the Lakers' won with 122-104 points. Previously the highest record was made by Elgin Baylor with 71 points and Kobe was the second-highest scorer in the history of NBA games. The first high scorer was Chamberlain and he scored 100 points in 1962. The case of Chamberlain and Kobe was quite different as Chamberlain had many shots created and assisted by his team members. But Kobe was recognized for creating his shots and usually he did not like when he was assisted to make the shots. Chamberlain's time was different and then scoring high was comparatively easy than it was for Kobe.

Kobe made another record in this same game. Earlier Baylor and Chamberlain scored 45 points in 4 consecutive games. Kobe was the only person in his generation and fact since 1964 to achieve this honor. This month was very well for Kobe as he achieved many things in this same month. In this month Kobe's average score per game was 43.4 points.

In NBA history, Kobe's score was considered to be the 8th highest single month. This was highest than all other NBA players except Chamberlain and it was because of Kobe the Lakers earned the tag of most points (40) per game. He also earned most point scores with 2,832 and was awarded the League's scoring title with 35.4 points per game. He became the 5th player in NBA history to average 35 in one Season. If that was not enough to boast his spirit, he had another event in his bucket. In 2006, Kobe was voted and got 4th position in NBA Most Valuable Player Award. It made him an irresistible player in NBA and no matter whether you hated him or disliked him but you could not overlook him or deny his successful track records!

2006-2007

Kobe's first-ever high school Jersey number was 24 and later he switched it to 33. For 2006-2007 Season, Kobe wanted to switch his number back to 24 again. As a Lakers member, he had the number 8 but Kobe always liked the number 24. When he started his playing as a rookie he wanted the number 24 but it was not available, so he was assigned with 33. This was said by himself in an interview with TNT that he would love to switch back to the number he played with in the beginning of his basketball playing days.

Kobe in the Adidas ABCD Camp wore jersey number 143 but since it was a campaign, he did not bother to changing it to his likings.

In this season the Lakers' were having an upper hand when they faced Phoenix Suns. Their Playoffs were so good that they got an easy lead with 3-1. In Game 4, Kobe shot a game-winning shot but despite Kobe had performed very well but the Suns ultimately won the final game. The final score was 126-118. Kobe scored 27.9 points per game and in Game 6, the Lakers' scored 50 points but still lose the game. This loss for the Lakers' led the sports experts to criticize Kobe for taking only 3 shots in the 2nd half. People always desire more from Kobe and ultimately after a bad performance of the team, Kobe is the one who gets the blame on his shoulders!

Despite losing the game, depending on Kobe's performance alone, he was again selected for the 9th appearance for the NBA All-star Game. February 18, he scored 31 points with 6 assist points and got 6 steals and earned the All-star Game MVP award for the 2nd time. But good news did not come alone in his life; it brought with it a bad news of the court incidents again.

On January 28, they faced San Antonio Spurs and his performance was well in the game. He was supposed to make a jump winning shot but he made a terrible foul which led him to get suspended.

Kobe hit the striker from the Spurs, Manu Ginobili's face with his elbow and it was done purposefully. The Lakers' were supposed to face New York Knicks at Madison Square Garden. But due to the foul Kobe made in the previous game, he was suspended for this game. The authority explained that Kobe's movement in an unusual motion backward is suspicious.

In that same year, on March 6, Kobe repeated this unusual motion but only this time Kobe stroke Marko Jaric from Minnesota Timberwolves. It was very evident that Kobe intended to hurt Marko and NBA noted it down properly and handed over Kobe's 2nd suspension on March 7. Kobe had to sit out from another game and it did cost a lot to the Lakers' to lose a teammate like Kobe for such a crucial game. All these suspension notices did not teach Kobe any lesson as again On March 9, a game with Milwaukee Bucks, Kobe repeated the same act of Type 1 flagrant foul and this time Kobe elbowed Kyle Korver. Kobe could not control his anger during those matches and it did cost Kobe in terms of damaging his appearance and the team to lose without their best player.

On March 16, The Lakers' played with Portland Trail Blazers and Kobe's playing was tremendously good. Kobe made a high score of 65 points and this was the highest score in the Season. This win helped the Lakers' to remove the tag of losing 7 Games at a straight. In Kobe's 11 years career, this was his 2nd best score. In the next game, the Lakers' faced Minnesota Timberwolves and in this game, Kobe scores 50 points. Kobe was in a very good state of his basketball career and in the next Game with Memphis Grizzlies and he scored 60 points. With these three games, Kobe made another record and he scored 50 plus points in a row for three games straight. Michel Jordan did this back in last 1987 and Baylor from the Lakers also had a record of scoring 50 plus points for three games in a row. For Baylor, it happened back in 1962.

Kobe was not done and he kept his high performance going on. In the next match with New Orleans or the Oklahoma City Hornets Kobe again scored 50 points. This score also made NBA history and he was the 2nd player to achieve scoring 50 points in a row for the 4th time in one Season. The first player was Chamberlain to make this record. This year was glorious for Kobe with many achievements in his bucket and by the end of the Year, Kobe had 10 games where he scores 50 or above 50 points. In that very year, Kobe won the straight scoring Title and Kobe's fan base had an increase too. Kobe's Jersey's were always sold out in the USA and CHINA.

His Jerseys were the number one selling Jersey's in those two countries during 2006-2007 Season. People started to assume the increase in the Jersey sell must be due to the new number Kobe choose for him. Kobe was still facing court calls but it did not put an effect on Kobe's basketball ground.

2007-2008

2007 started with a flimsy beginning for the Lakers and despite Kobe's last Seasons significant performances and NBA records, this year Kobe was having mental issues with Lakers' team members. He in an interview with ESPN on May 7 told them he would like to be traded if Jerry West does not join the Lakers'. But later Kobe denied that he would not like to be traded and he only confirmed that he wants Jerry West to join the Lakers' to benefit the team.

In only three days, Kobe again talked about his trading in a radio interview with Stephen A. Smith. In the interview, Kobe blatantly expressed anger for some Lakers team members who blame Kobe for O'Neal's departure from the team. O'Neal was also very good performance and a significant member of the Lakers. So it is very obvious some team members should miss O'Neal even after a long time. Kobe could not take the blame on his shoulders, so he expressed that he should be traded. For Kobe, it seemed, if the Lakers trade Kobe for someone better than him, the Lakers team member may stop blaming Kobe for O'Neal's departure.

On that very day, within three hours of the radio interview, Kobe had a conversation with Coach Jackson. Jackson could calm Kobe down and make him understand how important he is for the Lakers. Kobe was tamed and for that time the thought of trading was put off by him. Kobe again made a flimsy statement and this time it was a video amateur interview. Kobe boldly stated All-star Jason Kidd should join the Lakers and center Andrew Bynum should be traded with him. This statement made Andrew Bynum furious and sad at the same time. You would feel bad too when you know your team member whom you are sharing a team game with does not want you in the ground. This type of statement affects the game too.

The year 2007 had some ups and downs but as far as Kobe's performance goes in NBA, it was on a high. Kobe became the youngest NBA player to get 20000 points in the history of the NBA. He was only 29 years 122 days at that time. He achieved this in Madison Square Garden. The Lakers were pitted against the New York Knicks. Kobe scored 39 points with 8 assists and 11 rebounds. LeBron James was the one who broke the record later. On March 28, although the Lakers did lose a game with Memphis Grizzlies Kobe scored 53 points and 100 rebounds. This score was the Season's high score.

Kobe had an injury on his shooting hand. It was in his small finger. This issue is termed as a tear in the collateral ligament. This is an avulsion fracture. With this injury, Kobe managed to make this NBA record. No wonder why Kobe had a large fan following! Kobe's injury was caused during a game on February 5, 2008. Kobe should have gone for surgery and take rest until his hand recovered completely. But Kobe did the opposite. He played about 82 games of the Season. Kobe was very proud that he is putting off his surgery for the Laker's sake. He also was stating that he rather put off any type of surgery until the Olympic game is over. This shows how passionate and dedicated Kobe was for basketball and the Lakers.

He was not careless about his injury entirely and he knew he and the medical staff of Lakers' have to monitor the state of his finger constantly. With every game, Kobe and the medical staff were anxious about the hand injury. In September 2008, Kobe made the final decision that he will have any surgery on his finger.

Later the Lakers faced a game with the Nuggets and in this game Kobe significantly got aided by All-star Pau Gasol. Pau Gasol was traded to Lakers and together they reach a sky-high score. Kobe led the Lakers' and scored 57-25 so the Nuggets had it pretty rough. The Lakers' took them outright in the first round. Finally, on May 6, 2008, Kobe was the official League's MVP and Kobe was proud, honored and more importantly happy that all his work since 1996 has paid off. He was very proud to represent the city and the organization.

Kobe received the MVP award from David Stern, who was the NBA commissioner at that time. David praised Kobe a lot while giving the award and he was not at all surprised that Kobe received the award. According to David, Kobe deserved it as he always played well and this season was better than all the Seasons. On May 8, 2008, Kobe became the first member to get selected in the All NBA Team and the decision was quite unanimous. This happened for the 6th time in his NBA career and it had continued for 3rd straight Season. Kobe also joined the NBA All-Defensive First Team and with him, there was Kevin Garnett. He scored 52 points, and this earned Kobe 8th selection.

For the Lakers' 2007-08 was regular Season and they scored 57-25 points in the Regular Season. The Lakers' became first in the Western Conference and this win led the Lakers' to go straight for the first match with the Nuggets. In Game 1, the Lakers' scored enough to be safe to go forward and Kobe scored 32 points and he scored 18 points in the last 8 minutes of the game. Lakers win made the Denver fall out of the playoffs and in the next round, in Game 1, Kobe again scored well. He scored 38 points with the Jazz and the Lakers were fortunate enough to win the next game too. But in Game 3 and Game 4 the Lakers met unfortunate events as they lost both the games.

Kobe did his best and put forward 33.5 points per game but Kobe's input was not enough to bring a win for the Lakers. The Lakers; did win the next two games and this win led the Lakers' to go to win the semi-finals too. The Lakers' managed to win the semi-finals and the game was held at the Western Conference where the Lakers' face San Antonio Spurs in the finals. The Lakers' stool the semifinals in 5 games and for the finals, Lakers' faced Boston Celtics where Kobe was facing the finals for the 5th time. But this was the first time without having O'Neal in the Lakers. But the Lakers could not see victory this time and they lost to the Celtics in six games.

2008-2009 (NBA Finals MVP Trophy)

In 2008-09 Season Lakers starting of the year was quite good as the Lakers won 17-2 which led them to achieve a record. This record was for winning the most games during the start of a Season and by the end of the year, during December, the Lakers' got themselves a record of 21-3. Kobe again got selected for the All-star Game and this time he was assigned to start the game. It was his 11th consecutive selection and in December, Kobe won the titled Western Conference Player of the Month. Later next month, in January, Kobe was entitled Western Conference Player of the Week trice. These achievements were very delightful for Kobe and they only increased his passion for basketball.

On February 02, 2009, Lakers had a game with the New York Knicks and it was held at Madison Square Garden. Kobe snatched another record for him where he scored 61 points and it was the highest score ever in Madison Square Garden. Kobe again did well in the 2009 NBA All-star Game and there Kobe managed to get 27points with 4 rebounds and 4 assist points with 4 steals. This significant performance earned Kobe the title of All-star Game co-MVP and this award Kobe shared with his former Lakers teammate, O'Neal. There was good news for the Lakers too as the Lakers managed to snatch another NBA record. In the West, the Lakers score was the best record and they finished the season with 65-17.

LeBron James was voted first for the MVP award and Kobe was the runner up with which Kobe was pretty satisfied with! Then for the 7th time in Kobe's NBA career, he was picked for both All-Defensive First Team and All-NBA First Team. This direct pick gives reassurance of all the awards, titles and love of the audience for Kobe.

Later in the Playoffs, The Lakers faced Utah Jazz and beat them up successfully in five games. Then they faced Houston Rockets and beat them up in seven games and the two-round opening was good for the Lakers. In the Western Conference Finals, the Lakers faced the Denver Nuggets and the win was clear and the Lakers found their way to the NBA finals again. This was happening for the second time where the Lakers earned a straight trip to the NBA finals. In the NBA finals, the Lakers faced Orlando Magic and this was a good play for the Lakers and they won the championship. This win gave 4 championships in Kobe's NBA resume. The championship also earned Kobe the NBA Finals MVP trophy and this was his first MVP trophy and he was on cloud 9 for it. Kobe averaged 32.4 points in this series with 7.4 assists points and 5.6 rebounds. He also got 1.4 steals and about 1.4 blocks.

Since 1969 NBA Finals Kobe was the only player to get 32.4 points in the final series with 7.4 assists. West made the record in 1969 and afterward, only Kobe could get this glorious score. Kobe managed to get another record for him where he scored 30 points on average with 5 assists and 5 rebounds. This was the highest for a title-winning team and was done by only Jordan in the past. People in the NBA history always compare a rising star with Jordan and for Kobe to achieve what he had achieved earlier is remarkable.

2009-2010

This Season was also glorious for Kobe as On December 4, 2009, Kobe scored six shots that were game-winning. These included a one-legged 3 pointer and a buzzer-beating. The game was against the Miami Heat and the audience, the coaches and including Kobe admits it was a very lucky shot.

One week later after this lucky shot and game, Kobe faced an unfortunate event that was not so lucky for him. The Lakers faced Minnesota Timberwolves and Kobe injured his right index finger. Kobe suffered from a hand injury in the past too and with several contemplations on getting surgery, he finally decided to avoid surgery for it. This time too, Kobe did not take the injury seriously and he kept playing as opposed to taking any rests.

Just five days after he played another game with the Milwaukee Bucks and in the game, Kobe missed an opportunity in regulation. But in the overtime game, Kobe managed to make a game-winning shot. In this Season Kobe managed to snatch another NBA record and he was the youngest to achieve 25000 points in his career. He was only 31 years 151 days old at that time and this record surpassed Chamberlain too. Earlier Kobe broke many records but could not manage to surpass Chamberlain, so this time the joy of breaking the record doubled.

Later in a game with Sacramento Kings Kobe again made a game-winning shot. Earlier West was the greatest scorer in the Lakers team but Kobe surpassed him in this Season. With this good news came another bad news as Kobe had an ankle injury. Kobe was sidelined for five days and Kobe returned after five days in a game with Memphis Grizzlies. Kobe shot a three-pointer which gave them a lead and there were only four seconds left before Kobe could make the three-pointers shot. Two weeks after this match the Lakers played with Toronto Raptors and Kobe for the 6th time made a game-winning shot for the Season. Anyone who looks at these fascinating game winning shots would admit, it would have been rather difficult for the Lakers to win without Kobe's present in those games.

On April 2, 2010, it was time to renew the contract with Lakers again and this time Kobe signed the contract for three years and it was worth $87 million. Kobe was struggling to stay fit this year and as much as he would like to contribute to the team, he could not due to the knee injury and the right finger injury. He had to miss out on four games in the final games and throughout the Season Kobe suffered from many injuries. He would continue to play until he could not function in the basketball ground properly. This "not resting when he should" made his injuries last longer and in total Kobe had to miss nine games in this Season.

The Playoffs started and Lakers began their game with Oklahoma City Thunder and the Lakers swept them away in six games. In the second round, the Lakers faced the Utah Jazz and defeating them was also easy for the Lakers. In the Western Conference Finals, they faced Phoenix Suns and in Game 2, Kobe set another career-high score of 13 assists. Magic Johnson, in 1996, scored 13 assists points but no other Lakers managed to do it other than Kobe. The Lakers won all six games and this led them to win the Western Conference Finals. Then they went to the NBA Finals and this was happening for the straight 3rd time.

In the NBA Finals, the Lakers met the Boston Celtics to whom they lost the 2008 championship so they had unresolved history together which could only be sorted in the basketball court! Kobe managed to score 6 for 24 points from the field and they won the championship in game seven. Kobe scored 10 in the fourth quarter and he had 15 rebounds. This was the 5th NBA championship in Kobe's career and for the second consecutive year, Kobe got awarded for the NBA Finals MVP. They also made a record of winning Game 7 in the NBA finals against Boston Celtics. Kobe had the flavor of winning championships in the past but this win was best amongst all.

Chasing The 6th Championship

Chasing the 6th championship was not only important for the Lakers but also for Kobe as he wanted to match his game stat with Jordan. You cannot blame him for it as any basketball player would always dream to be on the same level as Jordan. The beginning of 2010-11 was good for the Lakers as they won eight games in a row but in the 9th game, the Lakers faced Denver Nuggets and Kobe snatched yet another NBA record in his bucket. This time Kobe grabbed the youngest NBA player to get 26000 career points. Since January 21, 2009, Kobe reached his first triple-double and on January 30, 2011, a match with the Celtics, Kobe became the youngest NBA player to acquire 27000 career points.

The Celtics and the Lakers had a history together and both teams are super strong and devoted and they seem to always neck to neck competition. On February 10, 2011, they had a game together and the Lakers snatched the victory with 92-86 points. Kobe successfully managed to score 20 points, and this win was against one of the league's top 4 teams. Kobe managed to get selected for the All-star Game for the 13th times straight. This was the season of wins as he also got the most votes and he received his 4th All-star MVP award. This time the authority tied the award with Hall of Famer Bob Pettit.

If you think Kobe is done with achievements in this Season, you are wrong! He also moved forward from 12th position to 6th position surpassing Oscar Robertson, John Havlicek, Hakeem Olajuwon, Dominique Wilkins, Moses Malone, and Elvin Hayes. He averages 20 shots per game which is comparatively the fewest since his stat in 2003-04 Season.

Kobe was great in his tactics and tricks in the basketball ground but when he lost his temper, he was not reluctant to show it too. On April 13, 2011, he made an abusive gay slur to the referee Bennie Adams. Kobe was upset with him regarding their previous match and the gay slur was an outburst of it. NBA did not tolerate such a childlike attitude coming from such a legendary NBA player. NBA fined him $100,000. Kobe was quite criticized for this act and the Human Rights Against Defamation marked Kobe's act as disgraceful.

Kobe was well aware of the issue and his faults in it and out of anger he said and did something that he regretted later. He explained to the press that he wished to talk it out with the Gay community and Kobe did apologize for his childlike behavior and was rather regretful about it. Kobe and the Lakers arranged a public service announcement where both Kobe and his teammates denounced his behavior.

Due to Kobe's behavior, the public shaming or the stress, all of it may have got into the Lakers head and they could not focus on the playoffs as they did in the past. In the second round of the playoffs, the Lakers met a sad ending with the Dallas Mavericks.

Surpassing Jordan's Score

Kobe still had his injuries and this time he could not put them off anymore. He had to treat it and he went to Germany for it. He received Orthokine on his ankle and knee. Jackson who was retired became the offseason coach for the Lakers during this time. For Kobe, the Season started with a wrist injury and with his wrist injury, he still managed to score 48 points with the Suns. His good score kept with him for the next three games too, 40, 42 and 42. This happened for the 6th time where he scored 40 plus points in four consecutive games.

2012 NBA All-star Game was glorious for Kobe as he finally could surpass Jordan's score in an All-star Game. He scored 27 points and became the career scoring leader but the Game was not as easy to win and Kobe was injured again with a foul made by Dwyane Wade. He broke his nose and he had a nasty concussion. This was not enough but in April Kobe had more injuries to stop him from playing. This time he injured his left chin and he had to miss seven games. The good news is he could make a return for the last three games and the last game was with Sacramento and Kobe had to score 38 points if he wanted to surpass Kevin Durant. Kobe was wise enough to omit the idea of opting for the third possible NBA scoring title.

Again in the second round of the playoffs, the Lakers met their sad ending against Oklahoma City Thunder and they lost five games and this was the second time in a row to lose the playoffs in the second round. From becoming champions for many times in a row to swept off in the playoffs rounds is very disheartening and almost impossible to carry the burden with a positive note but the Lakers' did not have a choice but to wait patiently for better days to come.

2012-2013 (Misfortune Again For The Lakers)

The Lakers had point guard Steve Nash and center Dwight Howard joining them in this season. On November 2, 2012, the Lakers played with the Clippers and Kobe's performance was good as he scored 40 points and 2 steals. Magic Johnson was the highest career leader in steal but Kobe managed to surpass him in this game. With all Kobe's effort, it was not enough to bring a win for the Lakers and they lost the game and gave a poor score of 0-3 starting the season. This never happened before in 34 years of Kobe's NBA career.

The scores were so poor that they had to fire the coach and Brown was replaced with Mike D'Antoni who happened to be Kobe's father's colleague. They both were star players and Kobe knew him as a child and this time as a coach they created a special bond between them.

Youngest To Score 30,000 Points

Kobe made another history by grabbing 30000 points and he was the youngest to achieve it in the league. It happened on December 5, with a game against New Orleans and before Kobe, Jordan, Chamberlain, Karl Malone, and Kareem Abdul Jabbar made it to the Hall of Fame with that score. Kobe was the 5th person to achieve it and he was the youngest too.

Kobe made another record by scoring 30 plus points against the Charlotte Bobcats and this was his 30+ score in seven consecutive games. After turning 34 Kobe made the longest streak of scoring this high and the final score was 101-100 and all the members did significantly well. Later on December 28, the Lakers won with the Blazers and his winning streak reached 10. The score of the game was 104-87, which is quite impressive too but Kobe sat out the fourth quarter and yet managed to score 27 points. Kobe's performance always surprised people around him and despite having such unrealistic odds at times, he still could score and performed significantly well!

D'Antoni's Strategies

D'Antoni made a strategy to improve the Lakers game and placed Kobe to guard the best player from the team they are combating with. Kobe discovered his innate ability to play even better when he is defending a strong player as opposed to a weaker opponent. This motivated Kobe further to improve his game and train harder to be the best at his game.

The start of the season was rather upsetting but Kobe leads the league with good scores. D'Antoni put Nash as a spot-up shooter and put Kobe as the primary facilitator on offense. This helped Kobe to achieve the highest assist points, 39 in his career. In March the Lakers had two important games and they stool victory in both. Kobe, as usual, did good and scored 40 points in each game. He had back-to-back 10 assists per game which made an NBA record. West got this in 1970 and afterward, Kobe was the first Lakers to do it.

In the 8th and final playoff, the Lakers struggled to secure their position and Kobe had several injuries yet he played 48 minutes per game. For Kobe, there was another career-high waiting for him on April 10, 2013. He scored 47 points, 5 assist, 8 rebounds and 3 steals which never happened in the history of NBA games before. The joy could not sustain for long as on April 12, Kobe suffered from another severe injury. They had a game with the Golden State Warriors and Kobe fell injured with torn Achilles tendon. This injury was crucial for Kobe as he was playing 40 minutes in seven consecutive games and he could not continue his glorious journey due to the injury that he no longer could avoid. He was only 34 years old but he was averaging 38.6 minutes in the last six years. The only person who was averaging more minutes than Kobe was Portland's rookie Damian Lillard.

The general manager knew about the injury's severity so he mentioned it to Kobe and showed his concern. But Kobe was determined about pushing the Lakers' performance for the Playoffs. He was not ready to decrease his minute in the game as he knew it would de-motivate the entire Lakers team. For the team's sake, he continued with his minutes despite the severe injury. Kobe had to take surgery to fix the tear on April 13 and everyone assumed Kobe would miss out on approximately six to nine months as the surgery required Kobe to take rest. Kobe's season ended with 27.3 points, 5.6 rebounds, 6 assists, and 46.3 percent shooting. This score is not as significant as his last few seasons but different critiques including The New York Times described Kobe's leading the team is one of the finest performances of his career. Even in this season with his injury, he managed to reach 40 points eight times. His assists skill was described as "magic mamba" and it was inspired by Magic Johnson.

One miraculous thing that everyone noticed is despite Kobe's injury, his field goal percentage went on top since 2008-09. His assists points became the second-best of his entire NBA career. The team ended up with the final 45-37 score in the season and it was on the seventh ranking in the West. The playoffs did not serve the Lakers well as they were missing their best player and they faced San Antonio Spurs. They lost in the very first round of the playoffs and gone out off the playoffs in four games.

2013-2014 (Years With More Injuries)

2013-2014 began successfully but Kobe could not join the team right away due to his health conditions. Kobe could resume his practices in November 2013 and he signed his contract with the Lakers for another 2 years which was worth $48.5 million. Kobe was the highest-paid player of the League and he was criticized for this even though he signed a discounted deal; people still thought he was charging too much. He could receive a contract worth $32 million per year but he preferred the earlier one.

The value of the contracts was a polarizing topic for everyone as the supporters would say the pay was not good enough and it was not valuing the talent of the NBA stars. On the other hand, the detractors focused on providing financial freedom to the entire team and less money to one or two-star players.

Kobe could not play the first 19 games of the season due to the after surgery rest. Kobe joined the Lakers on December 8 and Kobe snatched a season-high score of 21 points on December 17. They played with the Memphis and the winning score was 96-92 and in this game, Kobe again suffered from an injury on his left knee. It was lateral tibial plateau fracture and for this, the coach had to sideline Kobe for 1.5 months. Kobe could play only six games after he resumed playing in the team. In those six games, Kobe averaged 13.8 points, 4.3 rebounds, and 6.3 assists.

Kobe was sidelined but he had a large fan following and his fan-voted him to start 16th All-star game. Deep down inside, Kobe was feeling very disappointed over his injuries and his performance in the Season. He was having mixed feelings on being voted to start the game since his performance was not satisfactory to himself. He could not help but doubt himself whether or not if he deserved to start the game. Due to his knee injury, he could not play the game anyway so his dilemma was put to rest.

On March 12, 2014, the Lakers' decided to rule out Kobe from the season and this decision was needed for Kobe to take rest properly and the teammates to focus on the game with full concentration. With Kobe hanging on the sideline, everyone hoped maybe Kobe would become active and fit to give his 100%. With this false hope, the teammates could not concentrate whole-heartedly in the game. They had to rule out Kobe for the betterment of the Lakers team and during that time, the Lakers had the worst score in the Western Conference. It was a disappointing 22-42 score and Kobe was almost heartbroken for it.

Earlier in 2005, the Lakers missed a playoff and again in 2014, they repeated their sad history of missing another playoff. The Lakers finishing score was 27-55 which was as disappointing as missing the playoff itself.

2014-15 (Kobe's Glorious Return)

With many injuries and disappointment in the last season, this season gave so much back to Kobe. Kobe managed to break many records and snatched many wins for the Lakers in the 2014-15 season. It was Kobe's 19th season playing with the Lakers and by that time their coach D'Antoni was replaced with Byron Scott who was Kobe's former teammate.

On November 30, 2014, the Lakers faced the Toronto Raptors and won with a 129-122 score. Kobe was fortunate enough to make his 20th triple-double in this game and his score was 31 points with 11 rebounds and 12 assists. This made another NBA record of achieving 30 points, 10 assists, and 10 rebounds as the oldest player in NBA and Kobe was 36 years old at that time. Kobe could snatch himself both the youngest and oldest scores in many categories which reassure his skills as a basketball player.

On December 14, the Lakers played with Minnesota and their winning score was 100-94. Kobe was ranked 3rd in the all-time leading scorer in this game and he passed Jordan's score 32,292. For the first 27 games, Kobe averaged 26.4 points and he played about 35.4 minutes per game and it was a team-high score in the season. Despite playing so gloriously, Kobe suddenly became the worse of his career in one game with Sacramento. He scored 25 points but he had 9 turnovers and they lost with a score of 108-101. Scoring for Kobe became almost like an rollercoaster rise here and he himself could not decide how to improve this poor stat!

The Return Of The Injuries

The coach, Byron Scott made a bold move and he held out Kobe for the next three games. Kobe was also having difficulties with his injuries again as he had soreness in the knees, Achilles tendons, back, and feet. Scott knew Kobe would not speak up about his injuries neither he would voluntarily hold out to take rest. Scott decided he could put less pressure on Kobe and let him rest more so he can recover from the health issues.

Scott was feeling guilty that Kobe was taking so much pressure for the team with his injuries. There were three times when Kobe had to go over 40 minutes in a match. This put him in a bad shape slowly. Kobe started the season with such high enthusiasm and spirit, Scott felt very sad when he saw Kobe's health getting worse again. Scott innately blamed himself for overloading Kobe for the extra minutes in the games.

In this season Kobe could shoot only 37 percent from the field and the Lakers scored 8-19 which is rather poor if you see their history. After sitting out for three consecutive games, Kobe's second game with the Denver was good. The Lakers swept them away with a 111-103 score and in this game, Kobe had earned 23 points, 11 rebounds and 11 assists and this score led him to achieve multiple triple-double at the age of 36. He was the 3rd player in the league to achieve this glory. These were all good news but for some reason in Kobe's life good news always comes with a bad news. Kobe could not remain injury-free for long.

On January 21, 2015, Kobe again hurt his right shoulder and he had a rotator cuff tear while he was driving baseline. It was a game against the New Orleans Pelicans and he was attempting a two-handed dunk when he hurt his shoulder and he did not sit out the game either as always. He hurt his right shoulder, he was also a right shouldered person, and yet he returned in the game playing with his left hand. His passing, dribbling and shooting were rather exclusive even with the left hand. Before this shoulder injury occurred, Kobe rested for 8 games and Kobe had to take the surgery immediately and he could not wait for the season to end. His average in this season was 22.3 points but his shooting score was the lowest of his career, 37.3 percent.

After his season-ending surgery, everyone expected Kobe to return after nine months of rest. People deemed Kobe would be able to join the 2015-2016 Season from the beginning. Without Kobe in the team, the Lakers had the worse season of their career and they recorded as the lowest score and wins in a season with 21-61.

2015-2016 (The Last Season)

Kobe was supposed to rest and then come back in the preseason and everyone was eagerly waiting for Kobe to make a grand return on the ground where he belongs. Kobe's fortune was not good enough and he fell into a calf injury again. He had to miss two weeks of the exhibition games and Kobe was lucky enough to start the season as his 20th season with the Lakers. John Stockton was the only person to play in the same team for 19th times but Kobe did surpass him making his 20th time to play in the same team.

On November 24, 2015, Lakers had a game with the Warriors and the game was rather unfortunate for the Lakers as they fell to 2-12 with the loss with the Warriors scoring 111-77. Due to the calf injury, Kobe in 25 minutes scored only 4 points and the situation was so dire that he shot 14 times and scored 1 score. Earlier Kobe never had such poor shooting score and this broke a record but in a very disappointing way. Even in his lowest scoring history, he scored at least 5 shots in the past. This misfortunate event surpassed all of his previous bad performances.

Kobe knew his health condition is no longer supporting him in the basketball ground. He knew all the hard work he had put in his long career building a reputation, making his strong stat and all those NBA records would perish away with the horrible bad performances he was giving now. He saw it clear his NBA career can no longer continue with the numerous injuries he suffers in every season. It was a very essential and wise decision to retire from the NBA. Kobe decided that this Season should be his final. He officially announced on November 29, 2015, with *The Players 'Tribune.*

Kobe's career's last game was against his hometown team the Philadelphia 76ers. Kobe could not win his last ever game and lost with a score of 103-91. The game held on December 29, 2015. Who would have thought the start of such rookie with massive force would end in such bad loss. Everyone wishes to end his career with a game everyone would remember! Kobe's injury could not let him achieve that. Kobe broke so many records in his long basketball career but his last match was disappointing for himself too.

The Poem, "Dear Basketball"

Kobe wrote a poem showing his respect and his passion for basketball and the poem was titled "Dear Basketball" and it spoke out his heart out loudly. He mentioned to ESPN that this love is not something had he developed after he had joined the NBA. His father was a basketball player and his love was perhaps inspired by his father to a large extent. Since the age of six Kobe fell in love with this game and ever since then he kept developing his skills.

For someone who loves something so passionately and then to let it go is heart drenching. He cannot keep playing with all the injuries and skipping on several games to rest. He could not let the team down anymore and he could not face his lowest scores as opposed to making NBA records surpassing NBA legends like Jordan or Chamberlain.

Kobe poured his heart out in a letter which he addressed to the Lakers fans. This letter, they distributed before the Lakers played a game with the Indiana Pacers. It showed how down to earth Kobe was and how appreciative of the fans he was. Not everyone can be generous and appreciative of their fans when they reach a high status. When Kobe announced his retirement after the season ends, he was leading the team in each game with 16.7 field goal attempts. Kobe was playing 30.8 minutes per game which was second in ranking behind Jordan Clarkson. Due to his injuries, his scores were career-low of 15.7 points and his shooting was 31.5 percent. Everything collapsed for him in terms of assisting, shooting, scoring, stealing, etc.

Kobe knew about his weaknesses at that moment very well. He was not hiding anything from the press or his fans and he was true to his misfortune and his lacking skills. The strongest features of Kobe that everyone loved were no longer there and he himself acknowledged it quite well. He accepted all his declining skills in a press conference. He mentioned he was playing bad but he was trying very hard not to make it worse than what it is! He was doing everything of his ability and basically everything his physique would let him do, he was attempting it. But all of those hard work and effort were not shown in the basketball ground.

Kobe's Request On Avoiding A Farewell

Kobe made a request to his opponents of the NBA that no one should present him any gifts nor should anyone arrange any on-court ceremonies to honor him. Kobe was somehow struggling between whether or not to quit. He did not want any extra attention from anyone and hence he insisted on not getting any farewell and the hassle and arranged staged farewell gave him bad anxiety. After having many injuries over the years, Kobe's techniques and skills began to drop on the basketball ground which led the fans to boo for Kobe. The last match against the Sacramento left a hole in Kobe's heart. He heard so many curses and boos that the thought of staged cheers and farewell gave him anxiety and he mocked it by saying he would prefer boos over staged cheers!

Kobe's fan was not heartless and they did honor him with video tributes and fans gave him standing ovation to cheer him too. Earlier in his career Kobe was not always shown love, he did see respect from people more often but when he was leaving, everyone showed him how much they love him too. This made Kobe speechless, he was rather astonished.

On February 3, 2016, the Lakers had a game with the Minnesota Timberwolves and Kobe was fortunate enough to score seven three-pointers. He scored 38 points which were a season-high score and he made 14 points out of the teams' 18 points. The Lakers won the game with 119-115 score which ended their 10 games losing record at a stretch.

If they did not win this game, they would make the longest losing streak in their franchise history.

With all the lows happening in Kobe's life and in Lakers gaming history, Kobe managed to break yet another record. He became the 4th player to score 35 points, with 5 rebounds and 5 assists at the age of 37 in one match. In the 2016 All-star Game Kobe got the most votes with 1.9 million and the second-highest vote-getter was Stephen Curry with 1.6 million votes.

Kobe was moved to short forward in that Season and for this reason, for the first time, Kobe was assigned as a frontcourt starter. The last All-star Game for Kobe was back in 2013 and this was overwhelming for Kobe and he could score 10 points with seven assists and six rebounds. The West teammates wanted to feed him the basketball so Kobe could get another shot at the MVP award. But Kobe knew where he stood and he was not ready to feed the ball to earn the trophy.

The Season Finale

The season finale was on April 13, 2016, and the Lakers game was with Utah and Kobe did snatch the victory for the Lakers with his head held high. He scored 60 points which were the season-high score and in the fourth quarter Kobe also outscored the entire Utah team with 23-21. The winning score was 101-96.

At the age of 37 years 234 days, Kobe became the oldest NBA player to achieve 60 points in a game. This achievement in his last game was remarkable not only for the Kobe fan club but also for himself to boast his broken soul. Although, the Lakers' had the worse season-ending score of 17-65 which was a bummer but Kobe could at least take a deep breath and inhale for the new record he made.

National Team Career

For Kobe, getting picked for the national team at an early age was very overwhelming and the first-ever national pick was in 2000 where he had the opportunity to compete in the 2000 Olympics. Despite the vast eagerness to compete there, Kobe had to decline it for that year due to getting married. He prioritized his personal life here over his playing and you cannot really blame him for it as Marriage is also a big part of anyone's life. He had planned to get married during the off-season and if he went to the 2000 Olympics, he would not be able to hold the marriage ceremony properly.

Kobe was again picked to enter the 2002 FIBA WORLD championship and everything did not go according to the plan and Kobe could not play in this championship either. In the 2003 FIBA WORLD championship, Kobe underwent arthroscopic surgery for his knee and shoulder injuries. These surgeries also put him to rest so he could perform in this championship either.

In the next summer, Kobe was in the Olympic team but because of a sexual assault case, he was withdrawn from the team. For the 2006-2008 US Preliminary roaster Kobe and LeBron James were the first two picks.

The pick was made by Jerry Colangelo himself in 2006 but Kobe could not enter the 2006 FIBA WORLD championship either as he had to go for a knee surgery again. It seemed like there is always something there to stop Kobe from participating in those games.

2007 was the year when Kobe could finally start his real National team career and earlier it was only limited to getting picked but being able to perform in the basketball ground. Kobe was in the USA FIBA Americas Championship Team and in 2007 USA Men's Senior National Team. They finished a 10-0 score and earned a spot in the 2008 Olympics and they also won gold. Kobe was fortunate enough to start all the 10 games of USA's FIBA Americas Championship games. Per game Kobe averaged score was 15.3 points, with 2 rebounds, 2.9 assists, and 1.6 steals in the games.

Kobe got picked for the 2008 Summer Olympic on June 23, 2008 and he did get the opportunity to go to the Olympic before but everything did not favor him earlier, so this was the first time where everything was put into the right place and he finally went to the Olympics. Kobe scored a total of 20 points which also included his fourth-quarter 13 points and with six assists points in that game. The USA team won with the Spain team with a 118-107 score and it was on August 24, 2008, and they won a gold medal. The USA team won their first gold medal after the 2000 Olympics and Kobe averaged with 15.0 points with 2.1 assists and 2.8 rebounds in the 8th Olympic contests.

Since 2008, there was a gap for Kobe due to his injuries and surgeries and in the 2012 summer Olympics, Kobe was able to rejoin the USA team again. Kobe won another gold medal but this time he thought it would be wise to retire from the National team. Kobe faced three tournaments as a National Team player and won three gold medals each time and when Kobe was retiring his National team career, his score was 26-0.

Life after Basketball

Kobe fell in love with the game basketball since he was only six, so for him to retire from a 20-year career is unimaginable. People both his fans and detractors deemed that Kobe would be under depression after he retires but this was not the case at all. Kobe found his passion in something else other than sports! Being a father, he was also enjoying and embracing fatherhood more than ever after his retirement from the NBA, but he kept his passion alive in a new and creative way.

Kobe focused on producing and creating films after his NBA retirement and this was said in an interview with ABC NEWS one month after his retirement. He was starred on the cover of an eGame (2k17) of the Legend Edition and Paul George was the cover star of 2k17. After his retirement, to be featured as a Legend in an eGame surely put him in a good spark and this generation is crazy about playing eGames and the craze around Kobe is also huge. The creators successfully combined those two deadly combinations and referring to this eGame, He twitted that even if the black mamba is out, the "Legend" lives on. It is very true with his 20 years NBA career, he had made many records and snatched so many victories for the Lakers that this Legend will always live on people's hearts. This was the last video game Kobe appeared in but there were many NBA games where he appeared earlier in his career. He appeared there as the covered athlete in those games.

In 1998, Kobe Bryant in NBA Courtside got released and it was accepted well by the audience. Later next year, they released the game NBA Courtside 2: Featuring Kobe Bryant and then 2 years later in 2002, they released the game NBA Courtside 2002, and it also featured Kobe as the featured athlete. Then for three years, they did not release any game featuring Kobe but in 2005 they decided to launch NBA 3 on 3 Featuring Kobe Bryant. Then Kobe was featured in NBA '07: Featuring the Life Vol. 2, NBA '09: The Inside and NBA 2K10.

2019 was a glorious year for Kobe too as he was a global ambassador in China for the 2019 FIBA Basketball World Cup. It was an honor for him to go there and he was linked with China for many NBA and charity based programs. So for him, China had a special soft spot in his heart and he was thrilled to be receiving such an honor.

Starring on the cover of many magazines was not an unusual event in Kobe's life. But this 2k17 Legend edition was special and it did put a glow on Kobe's face. Some may argue that perhaps he was happy for the fairytale ending of his NBA career with 60 points in his last game. You decide which one you would like to believe, both are good news, and the Legend is happy, that is what matters!

The ABC News interviewer asked Kobe how he was doing one month after his retirement, and whether he was itching to get back into the basketball ground again! Kobe replied with a very cool remark that he is better than ever. He was fully enjoying his fatherhood, taking rest, enjoying a peaceful time with his friends and family and reflecting on his life. Some people thoughts perhaps Kobe is out of the limelight because he is antsy about his retirement, but Kobe cleared it out by saying he was very busy after retirement. Kobe also explained in the interview, since his father was also an NBA star, his dream was always to become as good as him. His dream did come true and people acknowledge Kobe as a Legend. Looking back on his career, he finds it blur, foggy and still spellbound by it.

He also told the news, that telling stories has been something he was always fascinated with. He would love to focus on a different type of people, around the world, living differently, balancing their joy and sorrow and bring it out in an aesthetic way on the screen so the world can see it. With this vision in mind, Kobe focused on producing and creating films. As a basketball player, Kobe was known to be notorious. He was always focused, always pushing hard and going the extra mile to improve him. As a producer, his plans were as determined as his last NBA career was.

The interviewer Michael Rothman could see Kobe's face lighting up when he started talking about telling stories and Kobe's Studio. It is not like Kobe began to see producing as a career option after his retirement. Ever since when he was a kid he envisioned telling stories and reaching it to the world on a grand scale. Also, he was going on a creative sector; his prime love for sport did not leave him. He wanted to enhance the beauty of sports and what sports can teach every human being. He wanted to connect the youth into sports and develop consciousness amongst them. The empowerment of a nation depends on the youth and he wanted to teach them the value of having good consciousness. He basically was looking for a way creative way to tell sports stories that evoke consciousness in youth.

In the interview, Kobe talked about his short films based on the poem he wrote "Dear Basketball" back in the 2015-2016 Season. The poem was distributed before an evening game to the audiences. Everyone knows how deeply felt that the poem was. Kobe poured his heart out in paper with that poem. A legend with gratitude is what makes Kobe special! John Williams, who was another legendary icon himself was supposed to assist him in this. John Williams created franchises like Jaws, Star Wars, etc. You know how good they did on the box office, and they were nominated for Oscars too.

Kobe had more projects in mind and that's why he had a smirk on his face and said everyone should wait to see what he comes up with next. He had a good vision of what he wanted to do, but it was a work under process, that is the reason he wasn't verbal about everything in that interview. The idea is to promote seeing the world with a zero-gravity lens. Kobe needed good writers to support his vision. For Kobe, the hardest part of developing his studio was finding the right person. Whenever he sat with someone who he may potentially hire for his studio, he had to have a positive vibe about them. The conversation between him and the candidate should flow in a direction that gives hope to Kobe that this person is right for the job. All of these seemed slightly difficult for Kobe as this was a new and rather grand project in his life.

Kobe also mentioned, his daily life has not changed miraculously after retirement. It is quite the same, the only difference was he did not have a strict protocol to attend to and he had more quality time to invest in his family. Kobe's life after retirement was still quite busy because he was constantly sitting with creators and discussing his vision. He was watching a lot of films, shows and he was reading too. He kept himself busy in learning the new interest of his life as a content creator. So his schedule was still hectic but basketball no longer kept him busy, a different medium did.

Kobe even sat with Stephen Spielberg who by the way- does not need any introduction. He told his story to Spielberg and hoped to collaborate with him on a great project. Kobe learned from speaking to these film icons, J. J. Abrams, Stephen Spielberg, Mark Parker, John Williams, and Jony Ivy. Kobe knew that telling his story to creative people and seeing their reaction could determine whether or not these stories are worth telling the world in a creative way. He knew it and he took the full opportunity every time he found a good creator. Kobe was not coy about his vision and stories. He wanted to share those sports stories in the light of perfection and he wanted those genius creators to scrutinize every bit of his content.

Kobe knew when something is edited, flourished and improved, it only gets better. He learned it from his own NBA life.

Kobe was also aware, due to his NBA star image; he had access to those legendary filmmakers. According to Kobe any wise person would take advantage of this fame and talk to them to improve the quality of his story-telling. This was definitely a wise move from Kobe. As a beginner, it is only obvious that he needed direction in many aspects and those experience heads could give him much insight inside the industry.

Kobe wanted his stories to be strong and they should make a mark inside people's minds. They cannot be a flimsy and onetime thing to remember. If the plot and the story-telling are grand, the impact in people's minds and hearts would be unforgettable too. To achieve it, Kobe needed critiques like those legends mentioned above. Kobe was not afraid or ashamed of admitting this. Brutally honesty is what you get from this 37-year-old mamba!

He wanted to build the youth, he wanted to evoke thoughts in them and he wanted to move the culture. To achieve all of those, the execution of his story cannot be anything less than great! Kobe also mentioned his target is not to aim for the Oscars much like most creators hope for. His aim was to introduce creative education and while he was doing it, if an Oscars knocks at his doorstep, he would not mind at all receiving it! Kobe knew if he can move people's hearts, only good would come from it.

Films

Although the very first film-related work in Kobe's life happened during his NBA career, there was no direct effort on Kobe's part in this film. In 2009, Spike Lee came up with a documentary film called, "Kobe Doin' Work". Just as the title suggests, it had in detail how Kobe functions in the NBA. It covered Kobe's chronicles of NBA 2007-08 Season. You would see all his tactics, moves and strategies in this documentary.

Kobe's first-ever self-made film was in 2017. He wrote and directed a short animated sports film entitled "Dear Basketball". This was a visual short film of his own poem he wrote back in 2015-16 Season. Since the poem was announcing his retirement, the emotions were very real and Kobe did not feel the need to hide it or be arrogant about it. He was calm and clear about his departure from the NBA. It had many emotions and gratitude towards the game and the audiences. He was honest about his feeling; he did not hide anything and held back in his animated film. All these were transformed into the screen beautifully by Glen Keane. John Williams did the music for this short film which was loudly appreciated by everyone too.

When the story is real, the emotion is heart-melting and the creators and contributes are fabulous, it bound to touch hearts. The short film also won many awards. In 2018, Kobe won the Academy Award for Best Animated Short Film. He was the only African-American to grab this award for the first time. Another record was, never before a former professional athlete had been nominated or won an academy award. This fabulous short film snatched another award entitled Annie Award in the category Best Animated Short Subject. It did not stop there, the film also won a Sports Emmy Award. "Dear Basketball" was produced in house, by Kobe's own company, Granity Studios.

With the very first creative project, Kobe managed to snatch three awards and became first in many categories. It was a proud moment for any African-American. People both inside and outside the industry have been lingering to see what Kobe does next.

Kobe was discussing his new project with Bruce Smith who is an animator veteran. Before the sad ending of Kobe's life, unfortunately, the project remained unfinished. It was only in conversation which was going six months prior to his accidental death.

For Kobe telling stories was a dream just like playing basketball as a professional. He loved his NBA career and even after his retirement, he was vibrant about his film making career. He was not someone who was only taking advantage of his fame, rather he was constantly learning the process of film making and story-telling. Everyone around him could see and notice the hard-work he was putting in to learn this new craft. He was reading, watching intellectual masterpieces. He was not letting go of any opportunities that come ahead of him to learn from others. He talked with good filmmakers frequently so he can understand what goes behind making a successful story. He knew it was teamwork and he focused on building his team strong. He knew the power of positivity and he wanted to hire people with good vibes and of course talent has to be the first norm.

He wanted to tell stories and inspire millions to do good and leave a legacy behind. Kobe could only tell one story successfully but it is safe to say his story did make a mark in everyone's heart. The short film was mind evoking, and not only the youth but any person can learn a lesson from it.

Books

As mentioned earlier, Kobe wanted to tell stories of inspiration and that can move culture, mind, and consciousness. What better way to tell stories than writing a book! After retirement, Kobe had time to reflect on his 20 years long NBA career and what didn't his career have? It was filled with so many ups and downs and all the injuries, all the unfortunate events, all the heart-breaks, and all the misunderstandings blur and fade away when you count the blessings. Kobe had many blessings as an NBA player, he grabbed so many records and award which made NBA history.

Kobe knew he had something to offer from his 20 years career to his fans and his experience in the form of a book is perhaps the best way to connect with the fans on a personal level.

The book, *"The Mamba Mentality: How I Play"* was a piece of art and it contained Kobe's ideology and tactics behind playing each game. How he approached every game was in detail in this book. The book also had photographs of Kobe playing in the basketball ground and with each photo, Kobe reflected on his experience, thoughts and the aftermath.

The book had an introduction written by Phil Jackson which was perfectly introduced Kobe's legendary game-play. The intro of the book would leave an itch inside you to read the entire book and learn about Kobe's tactics. The afterword of the book was done by Andrew D. Bernstein and Andrew was an American photographer who also did the photos of the book. Pau Gasol, Kobe's teammate, and a four-time NBA All-star added foreword for the book and it got published by MCD/FSG which was also a best-seller creating publishing company. So everything worked well for creating the book and Kobe had his fan supporting him in buying the book.

The book was not there only to make financial business, it was published to inspire the youth and give them first-hand gems from Kobe's 20-year long career. Wouldn't you feel happy to know a legend's thought process behind their game-play?

For a story-telling enthusiast, Kobe could not continue the blessing and he met with unfortunate death suddenly. He could tell his own story in his book but he wanted to do much more and he was working with Paulo Coelho, the Brazilian author who is known worldwide. They were working on a children's book and this time Kobe's focus was on underprivileged kids. For a legend, for a millionaire, for someone who has everything to think and care for the underprivileged kids are beyond admirable. There is something deeper to learn from this act of kindness and many of his close friends loved and learnt so much from Kobe's compassion towards the needy.

This project must have been successful and may have helped many kids to dream big and try to fulfill it with their effort but sadly the project could not see the light. Kobe died in 2020 and Paulo deleted everything related to this project because for Paulo, the logic was, the person who started it is no longer there, what is the point of publishing it now? Paulo did not mention anything regarding its length or title but it is quite saddening that the world could not see such beautiful work coming live.

Kobe wrote one book alone but he produced and co-wrote many novels (young adult) and they were published through Granity Studios. These are the ones that you can grab to get more insight into Kobe's mind and his ideologies.

"The Wizenard Series: Training Camp

Legacy and the Queen

Epoca: The Tree of Ecrof"

Kobe had his fourth novel ready but he could not see it published but the good news is *"The Wizenard Series: Season One"* is supposed to be live in somewhere in 2020. We hope that the world sees this beautiful work and appreciate the vision Kobe had in mind.

All this work after retirement shows how eager Kobe was to let out his creative side. Whatever happens; happens for a reason and if he had not had those injuries and surgeries, Kobe may not quit his NBA career and the world may never see his creative side. Basketball was always his first love but the creative field was something he also felt very passionately about. This is why he could create quality content within a short amount of time.

Music

It may surprise you that this legendary sportsperson could be a musician too? But in high school, Kobe was very attached to music and he was very interested in rap music and they had a rap group called CHEIZAW. The title is rather unusual but it was inspired by the famous 1979's movie *Kid with the Golden Arm*. CHEIZAW was a martial art gang name in the movie and their music was so good that they got signed by the renowned Sony Entertainment Company. It was a piece of great news for the rap group but their dreams were shattered when they found out the company only was interested in Kobe alone. They did not care about the rap group as a whole, but their target was to release a solo album of Kobe. The company knew about Kobe's basketball skills and his fame in the NBA so they did not care much about the music rather their target was to capitalize on the fame of Kobe.

Kobe performed solo in 1997's concert by Sway and King Tech and he performed a remix version of "Hold Me" which was originally by Brain McKnight. Kobe got much love for this performance but he was not seen doing another song any time soon.

Kobe made a special appearance in his teammate Shaquille O'Neal's 4th studio album Respect. His track was called "3 X's Dope" and it was a good collaboration too but Kobe did not have his credit in the album which made Kobe's fan question why proper credit was not given in the album. Kobe did not explain anything about this but the fans of Kobe was rather hurt about no giving him any credit for his appearance.

Kobe's music was slightly different and he did not do regular hip-hop, his music was slightly underground hip-hop which had its own audience but to broaden his audience Sony tried to push Kobe out of his under-ground hip-hop style as Sony wanted Kobe to do radio-friendly music.

In 1999, Kobe made another appearance with the famous girl group, Destiny's Child and that girl band was big and accepted by a vast number of followers. Appearing in their song was a good choice for Kobe and he appeared in their famous song's remix version, "Say My Name". It was the Maxi Single version of the song and with this appearance, Kobe's hopes on music career became bigger and he kept on trying to create more music with creative artists.

Kobe's very first debut album was supposed to release in 2000's springtime and he had supermodel Tyra Banks singing the hook of the song "K.O.B.E". It was the first single off the album and in January 2000, the single got released. It was performed in the NBA All-star weakness in the production and the song did not make any positive mark and rather receive much criticism. Sony sensed the negative reviews that single had and decided to drop the idea of the album since it did not seem like a good business plan to create the album. Sony dropped Kobe later in 2000 and Sony's President who initially signed Kobe for the album left Sony and the backers who supported Kobe initially also abandoned him after the first single.

Kobe could not wash off the music craze from his head completely so he kept on trying in the music industry. Kobe later co-founded a record label named Heads High Entertainment. Kobe's hope was high but it didn't follow through as planned as this record label had to close down within a year.

There was a big gap in his music creation due to not finding a good project and his love of music was always alive, but unfortunately for him, music was not doing any good both for him or the listeners. After a decade, in 2011, Kobe reentered into the music industry in a Taiwanese song called "The Heaven and Earth Challenge" which was pronounced as "Tian Di Yi Dou" in the Taiwanese language. It was a song by the artist Jay Chou. Kobe featured in the music video of the song too and the profit from the song and its download were donated entirely and it was donated to provide types of equipment for basketball facilities in different schools. The song had another purpose too, in China they used the song to promote the Sprite ad with which Kobe was affiliated with for a long time.

Kobe had the opportunity to make a mark on many musicians' hearts with his NBA records and his love for music. So artists like Lil Wayne gave tribute to Kobe with the song "Kobe Bryant" in 2009 and the song explained what a legend Kobe was in the basketball court. In 2010, Sho Baraka made another tribute to Kobe in his album "Lions and Liars". He entitled one song called "Kobe Bryant On'em" which explains Kobe's fantastic skills and life story in and outside the NBA. The gesture of honor is not given to many unless they earn it with their hard work and Kobe left behind a legacy when it comes to the NBA and because these artists loved him so much that they were inspired to create an entire song on Kobe. In a nutshell, Kobe's music career was not as great as he had hoped it would be but his love for music was always great.

Kobe's Business Strategies

Kobe was not only a legend in NBA but also he had a reputation as a brand builder and he was a good businessman with a clear vision of combing sports brands and promoted young sports brands. He was also a good coach for other players and sports companies and Kobe was wise enough to invest in the business world way ahead of his retirement from NBA. In 2013, Kobe Bryant and Jeff Stibel co-found the company Bryant Stibel and Jeff was the founder of the famous Web.com. Kobe was not only a co-founder in the company but also added his vision and executed many ventures successfully in the company. His entrepreneurship and investments led the company grow further and quicker.

Kobe learnt from his NBA legends who did not limit themselves in basketball alone. Star like Magic Johnson is a good example of expanding the career into multiple successful areas. Magic Johnson also founded a company in 1987, Magic Johnson Enterprise was a investor company. They invested in many sizable businesses and two of the very famous endeavors were New York's LaGuardia airport and Starbucks. Both did really well which proves they have a good strategy behind their investing.

Kobe invested in data companies, technology, and media and the company in 2020 holds $2 billion worth value. You would be surprised to know the game you play so often, Fortnite, your favorite player has invested in it. They also invested in website like Alibaba, which is one of the biggest wholesale online marketplaces in Asia that exists. They also invested in Dell, which is also a good technology brand worldwide. They also invested in The Honest Company where household items are sold and like the name, the service of it is also good and honest. Another successful investment is on Klarna, a digital payment company. Kobe and Jeff was wise enough to make at least 10 successful investments that worked for the long run.

Kobe talked about investing in true entrepreneurs that have something to offer to the people. Whenever they took up a new investment, they always looked at the people behind the project. If they find those people to be superficial, they never ventured in with them. If the people are honest and talented, that was the key for Byrant Stibel's company to invest in them. They knew getting returns and numbers are a big factor in this business but they also knew giving a hard-earned opportunity to someone who really needs it is also important. Kobe's focus was equally on building relationship with the investors. He knew there is no alternative to succeeding when you build good vibe in the working relationships and provide them with proper opportunity. When any entrepreneur does succeed in their ventures, it is good for Kobe's company too, he knew his success is tied up with their success.

Kobe had a great reputation as an athlete and it did not take him much time to build his persona as a brand builder. He was renowned for investing in startups and giving them a higher platform. This is what happens when you use your popularity to lift up others around you and this quality was admired by many and Kobe also had a neat eye on searching for real talent. He could sense somehow which startup would be good in the long run or which startup has more honesty in it.

Soon it became a trend when Kobe gives his approval to any startup, suddenly everyone in the sports industry began to take heed of their existence. It was a stamp of approval that they have potential and they can be trusted with good investments. So every entrepreneur used to take their chance with Kobe's company and get them interested in their business.

Kobe also ventures individually on different labels like Body Armor and it did significantly good and in 2018 they collaborated with the famous franchise Coca-cola. Michael Phelps the famous Olympics swimmer told in an interview that Kobe is a very interesting athlete with a good interest in the investments. He thought it must be very fun to dig into his brain and get the secrets to selecting such investments which bound to work. He takes a startup that no one knows and gives him this massive platform and within a few months, they become very big in the industry.

Michael Phelps also mentioned how he and Kobe know what it takes to get to the top level of any sports profession. It takes a lot of gut-wrenching effort, patience, fate, and skills to get there and sustain it. Many people go to the top levels and not many can sustain it too and those who can, are remembered with honor for the rest of their lives. He also mentioned it is good to have interests in other things than sports and life is all about challenges and mysteries. So when you know your strengths and weaknesses in your profession, now maybe it's time to find out what you can do outside of your profession! Kobe years before his retirement began to challenge himself with many other projects. He found it very satisfying to learn new things and invest in new categories. When the result was positive he patted on his back and when something unfortunate happened he looked for the next challenge. He was not a person to stop with any hurdles and he kept going forward with vision and ideas.

Black Mamba

Someone who did not follow Kobe closely may wonder with curiosity, why call a basketball player the "black mamba"? Before even starting to play for the NBA, Kobe was fortunate enough to sign a six-year-long contract with the famous sports gear brand Adidas and it was before the 1996-97 Season was about to begin. The contract was worth about 48$ million and they even came up with Kobe's signature shoe called KB 8. Another earliest collaboration was with Coca-Cola Company and Kobe promoted their Sprite soft drink and soon he became a renowned face for Sprite world-wide. He did many TV commercials for them and they became instant hits around the world.

Kobe also made endorsements for Upper Deck and it was quite successful. Kobe also affiliated with Spalding's to promote the new NBA infusion Ball. Nutella and Russell Corporation were also his famous endorsements and all of these glorious endorsements disappeared when the sexual allegations were put forward.

Kobe's earliest branding was with Nike. Back in 2003 Kobe signed his first contract with Nike. In that same year, Carmelo Anthony and LeBron James, these legends also signed a contract with Nike. This was positive in his career that he was doing the same thing as the elites. Michael Jordan retired in 2003, so Nike wanted to take players that would help them build their brand in the basketball industry. Getting those three elite players, Nike had the chance to establish their brand for the next decade properly.

After the sexual allegation, Nike did not abandon Kobe like the other companies, but for the sake of the disrupted image of Kobe, Nike decided to stop using Kobe's face to market their brand for that time. Kobe and Nike signed a contract of 40$ million before the sexual allegation happened. So Nike couldn't shut down Kobe entirely. Kobe's image did get better after two years when the woman did not follow through her case. Nike again began to use Kobe's face to promote their brand.

In 2008, Kobe was promoting Nike's special Hyperdunk shoes and to make the commercial epic and unforgettable, Kobe had to jump above an Aston Martin. Not just a simple car, but a speeding Aston Martin and everyone assumed the stunt was fake because it had many risks and it will violate the Lakers contract of Kobe. Later Kobe released Zoom Kobe IV which was his fourth signature collection with Nike and all of his collection did well and was very trendy. Because of the Kobe craze, Nike had to release one signature Kobe collection after another to meet the need of his fans. In 2010 they launched his 5th shoe collection which was entitled Nike Zoom Kobe V.

In 2009, Nubeo came up with a full proof plan to promote Kobe's fame with a luxury collection. Their collection featured watches that were both luxury and sports style and the collection was called, "Black Mamba collection". They were pretty expensive watches which started at the price of 25000$ and went up to $285,000. People who collect luxurious watches, these high-end prices are not an issue. What they care is about supporting their favorite athlete by buying his signature watches.

The beginning of 2009 was special for Kobe for another reason too and in February, Kobe was on the cover of the ESPN magazine. Surprisingly the reason behind Kobe being on the cover was not for his NBA career or any game, but for the fact that he was a fan of FC Barcelona.

Kobe had many endorsements but still in 2007, it was estimated that he earns 16$ million in a year and It was an estimation done by CNN. Within just 3 years in 2010, Kobe was one of the highest-paid players in the world and his earnings were about 48$ million per year.

He was only behind Tiger Woods and Jordan and it was a list made by Forbes and he ranked third in that list. He was the highest-paid athlete, but his money was going in the right places and he was not a fan of luxurious life so to speak, he had his private helicopter to go to events and games but he was not a spending fanatic just because he was a billionaire. In 2013, Kobe ranked as the 5th highest-paid athlete in the world and he was only behind LeBron James, Lionel Messi, Floyd Mayweather, and Cristiano Ronaldo.

Kobe began to break more records and increasing his stat in the NBA and his relationship grew more with Nike because of his success stories in the NBA. Nike focused on Kobe's popularity and releases many shoes and other sports gears giving tribute to Kobe. This helped Kobe's fans to grab all his gears and support him. Kobe was even brought to Nike's launch party for the new business strategies they are about to execute and it was an annual investor meeting and Kobe came to the stage with their CEO Mark Parker. This showed how important Kobe was for the Nike franchise.

Nike treated Kobe as an inseparable part of the Nike family and they even held a memorial day for Kobe after his retirement in 2016. Nike named that day, "the Mamba Day". Kobe had many endorsements when he was doing well in NBA, but in 2003 when the unfortunate sexual assault case arrived, all of his endorsements gone off except for Nike. Nike did not leave him even when everyone in the industry abandoned him. In 2017, Nike collaborated with Kobe, LA boys and girls club and launched the Mamba League. It was a basketball league where kids could enter the sports for free and this project helped a lot of youngsters to fall in love with basketball and improve their skills.

Kobe later created another golden opportunity for kids but this time it was not limited to only basketball. He founded the Mamba Sports Academy where they focused on improving kids' skills in different sports. The academy trained kids to compete on different levels in different sports. Kobe often spent time in this academy and he had many instructors who were highly professional and skilled. They trained kids with care and efficiency. Kobe always wanted to improve his academy and he kept everything up to date in the academy. Kobe's tragic death occurred during his travel to this academy through a helicopter ride.

Kobe had an active role in expanding the audience of the NBA by collaborating with Alibaba and NBA wanted to expand and build an audience in China. It was because Kobe collaborated with Alibaba first hand and released "Kobe Bryant's Muse" that the NBA got a line of fans cheering for them from China. They released the documentary in China through Tmall Magic Box TV.

Collaboration with Alibaba was rather successful and the youth of China began to enjoy Kobe's gameplay and started to follow his games. Their target was to bring more and newer avenue from China using Kobe's great performances and Alibaba sold many of Kobe's branded items in wholesale price.

The endorsements did not stop here and he had also collaborated with Turkish Airlines and Turkish National airlines, which was another hit. We all saw the enchanting TV commercial. The deal was finalized in December 2010 and Kobe shot the promotional film which aired in about 80 countries. This made his face recognized around the world even if they did not see basketball. It was not the film alone, but his face was used in digital, print media as well as in billboards.

Kobe was a fan of FC Barcelona and for him to star in a TV commercial with his favorite team member Messi was beyond a dream come true. It was a shot for the Turkish airlines back in September 2012 and both Kobe and Messi in the latest commercial of the airline works hard to impress a little kid. They both try to show their sports skills in front of the kid and impress the kid. Messi with his football does stunt that does impress the young child and Kobe with his basketball also enchants the kid. The plot of the commercial was refreshing and new and it appealed to all types of audiences world-wide. Kobe had a large fan following and Messi is one of the biggest football players out there.

He also invested in McDonald's, Nintendo and Sprite. All of these did well both for Kobe and the individual companies. These show how much of good picker he was when it comes to investing money.

Appearing on TV

Any sportsperson who does well in his work gets some offers to work in the entertainment field. Kobe also had his share of "acting jobs" and his very first acting job was way back in 1996. Kobe appeared in an episode of the Sitcom Moesha and the series was based on an LA girl who is played by R&B singer Brandy Norwood. Kobe first met Brandy earlier in 1996 in an event of Nike's All-star basket game and they began to converse and had a good time together. They kept in touch with each other and in May 1996, Brandy went to Kobe's High School Senior Prom as his date.

Again in 1998, Kobe made another appearance in the Nickelodeon's hit comedy show *All That*. In this show, he portraits himself and did a good comedy episode and in 2019, Kobe again appeared in another comedy episode of MTV's ridiculousness.

In 2018, Kobe wrote a TV series that later became multi-seasoned called "Detail" and it was for ESPN and ESPN+. Kobe also produced it and he himself hosted it and the thought process behind this series was to show every bits and piece of basketball in a broad-way. It showed how every basketball player functions in the game and it even explained their mental state before a big game. This show was basically a training slash entertainment series where people who love basketball and want to play it can learn from seeing it. It gave out many tactics and secrets of playing efficiently and you could see the search that went behind this series and the in-depth analysis of every episode.

The Sexual Assault Case

Kobe's life was upside down when the sexual assault case came out of nowhere. Kobe was a renowned NBA player in 2003, and he acquired many achievements in those few years of his NBA career. The sexual assault case damaged not only Kobe's NBA image but also his business endorsements, not to mention the disrupted image it made in his family too. Whenever something like this allegation comes forward, whether it is true or not, everyone starts to question everything. There are a few numbers of people to remain unmoved with the allegation news when it first came forward.

Back in the summer of 2003, Kobe got arrested by the Sheriff of Eagle, Colorado. A 19-year-old hotel employee filed a complaint against Kobe of sexually harassing her. The Sheriff arrested him to investigate the case further, and Kobe was suffering from a knee injury during that time and he had to take surgery to improve his knee's condition.

For the surgery, Kobe booked a hotel in Eagle County and it was The Lodge and Spa at Cordillera. The place where he was supposed to take surgery was nearby this Spa and the allegation was Kobe forcefully raped the hotel employee the night before his knee surgery. The act happened in his hotel room and Kobe did have a sexual encounter with that 19-year-old hotel employee but Kobe never admitted that it was a rape. He always stood strong in his statement although it was an adulterous encounter it happened in mutual consent. He never forced her to get involved with him.

When the assault first came into the public eye, most people believed it instantly without the final verdict from the court. Everyone was so disappointed with Kobe that they began to un-follow him and his reputation tarnished horribly and the endorsements he had for years also noticed the negative impact of the sexual allegation. They decided to drop off Kobe instantly to save their own company's reputation. No one wanted to be affiliated with a rapist or someone who has anything to do with sexual harassment. Only Nike was brave enough to continue the contract. All the other companies kept their distance from Kobe until the final verdict from the court which proved Kobe, not as a sexual assaulter.

Kobe's merchandise did really well in the market until this sexual assault case came into being. His Jersey's sales dropped so low that it did significant loss for the investors. No one wanted to work with Kobe and Kobe also missed an Olympic game for this Sexual Assault case. The 2003-04 Season for the Lakers' was also very bad due to missing so many games since he had to attend court calls quite often during that Season.

In September 2004, the final verdict from the court came off and Kobe's case dropped off. The accuser never showed up in the court to follow through the case and she for what reason never testified the trial. To improve his image as an NBA player and as a good businessman, he decided he would publicly apologize to the accuser. This was appreciated by his fans and teammates.

Kobe mentioned in his apology that from his side he deemed the encounter as consensual. But when he heard her attorney and listening to her testimony face to face, he realized perhaps she did not fully consent for the encounter like he did. The accuser filed a different case against Kobe after his apology. This time the matter was privately closed by the two parties. The media did not hear what they settled for but afterward, there were no controversies regarding this issue.

This dark episode in Kobe's like left a negative remark in his personal life too with his wife and the kids.

Wife and Kids

The Bryant Family had five members- Los Angeles Lakers basketball player, Late Kobe Bryant, who entered the National Basketball Association directly from high school, won 5 championship titles, played his entire 20-season professional career, two-time Olympic gold medallist and retired in 2016. His loving sweetheart, Vanessa Laine Bryant, aged 37 years along with her 4 other children- Natalia Diamante Bryant (19 years old), Late Gianna Maria-Onore Bryant (17 years old), Bianka Bella Bryant (3 years old), Capri Kobe Bryant (8 months old).

Going up the pedigree, the Bryant family also includes four more to add to the list. They were: Kobe's father, Joseph Washington Bryant who is nicknamed as "Jellybean". He is an American former professional basketball player and currently working as a coach. This explains how the family gets their gene for their passion for basketball. His wife, Pam Bryant and two other daughters Sharia Bryant and Shaya Bryant with whom Kobe Bryant was pretty close within his lifetime.

Coming back to Kobe's family, the Mexican American beauty, Vanessa Laine Bryant was born in Huntington Beach, California. She is of Mexican and Irish, English, German descent which gives her the spontaneous and diversified inherited traits which stand out her bold personality. Vanessa Bryant was a senior student at Marina High School when she was dating L.A. Lakers' legend. Back in 1999, when Vanessa was just 17 years old and Kobe was 21, they struggled to win their parents' consent. They were not supporting their young love but that did not refrain them from getting engaged 6 months after their first official date in May 2000.

She was compelled to finish her studies through homeschooling to avoid media attention. Vanessa is a former model and also starred in a couple of music videos and is known to make fewer media appearances than anticipated.

Vanessa married the legendary basketball player, Kobe Bryant on April 18, 2001, when she was only 18 years old. So lucky was she to have found the love of her life during her early years of adulthood. Their eldest daughter, Natalia Diamante Bryant, was born in 2003. Vanessa suffered a miscarriage in 2005 due to a case of ectopic pregnancy and in the following year, on May 1, 2006, she gave birth to Gianna Maria-Onore. 2011 was a dark time in the Bryant love story when Vanessa filed for divorce on December 16 that year. However, on January 11, 2013, she announced calling off their divorce and after three years their third daughter, Bianka Bella, was born in 2016. The youngest Bryant, Capri Kobe Bryant, was born on July 4, 2019. The couple was extremely focused on a family with a strong bond which resulted in Vanessa leaving her work and decided to be a stay-at-home mother fixing all her attention towards the upbringing of her kids.

The coping of Kobe Bryant and his baby daughter's passing away has not been exactly picture-perfect for Vanessa and her other three daughters. Growing up without their father by their side is fill in the blank which no one will ever be able to fill up at any point in their life. The family was so into athlete and sports which kept the Bryant family together with a team of spirit.

The half Latino, Natalia Diamante Bryant, their eldest daughter is an American volleyball player. She attended Sage Hill High School in Los Angeles, California. She has been under media scrutiny quite a couple of times from the national sports media in the US. Although Kobe Bryant is a famous basketball player, his eldest daughter does not share the same passion with him. But this goes without saying that she shares the passion of sports with him, in this case, it is the craze of volleyball for her. Natalia played volleyball in her early freshman season for Sage Hill. She was featured in 'The Washington Post'. Kobe's Principessa (lovingly called by her father), Natalia gained her recognition through various highlighted videos of her sporting skills posted online.

Late Gianna, born in Los Angeles, California, was raised with her three sisters. She held her father, Kobe was accountable for her inspiration towards playing basketball. Gianna Maria-Onore Bryant also lovingly nicknamed –Gigi and Mamacita (by Kobe) played basketball for the Mamba Sports Academy. She was coached by her father who won five NBA championships with the Los Angeles Lakers. 13 years old Gigi aspired to play college basketball at the University of Connecticut, where she attended the UConn, WNBA, and Lakers games with Kobe on a regular basis.

In an interview, Kobe mentioned how he always saw his baby Gianna as the female version of him. But nature had a different plan contrary to what the Bryant family aimed for. Gianna was on her way to the Camarillo Airport in Ventura County for a basketball game at Bryant's Mamba Academy in Thousand Oaks, where she met her tragic death and traveled to the afterlife with her father by her side this January on the 26th. Late Gianna Bryant had ambitions to join the WNBA as well. Kobe told Jimmy Kimmel in 2018 that whenever he and Gianna were out with the fans, they were always telling Kobe to get a boy to carry out his basketball legacy.

But Gianna always stood up to that idea and used to say, she is better off and it is not necessary to be a boy to carry out his father's legacy. She has got it all covered. Kobe was fascinated by his girl. This was published by the online version of the well-known newspaper brand, *The Sun*.

Just after the news of Kobe and Gigi's passing away, Vanessa Brant took her time to mourn and on January 30, 2020, she posted on her Instagram account about how the family is getting by at the moment. I read the post and immediately felt a wave of respect for her because of the approach she took to give a comprehensive account of her feelings and how she is dealing with them.

She was also thoughtful of the other families who lost their loved ones in the helicopter crash and what could be done by the people who were fans of the basketball champ to honor their demises. In an Instagram post, she mentioned being thankful to the million fans on behalf of the children and herself for their prayers and wrote how much the prayers meant to them. They were shattered with the demises of the other passengers who were in that helicopter crash and the way her family can relate to the families who have lost their beloved just like them. She kept on writing of how blessed they were to have Kobe and Gigi in their lives and it breaks their heart when they realize God took them from their lives earlier than was anticipated and how she wished they were by her side forever. She was thankful for all the love and support by the fans and appreciated privacy to allow their new reality to set in. She concluded her long post by requesting everyone to come forward and support the families who are at a loss like her due to this tragedy through the Mamba Sports Foundation.

Bianka Bella Bryant, the third child of the Bryant lovebirds is one of the sassiest according to her parents. It is not yet speculated whether she takes her interest after her dad and Gigi, or her mother or her sister.

Browsing through the basketball-star player's Instagram profile, this particular post caught my attention and tears swelled up in the corner of my eyes, it was about the announcement of baby Capri's arrival in 2019. The posts were written by them in January last year. In an interview on Extra TV in 2017, Bryant mentioned that Vanessa wanted a boy to add to their family. Despite that fact, God had a different plan and they welcomed their baby Capri in 2019.

The youngest Bryant, Capri does not understand what losing a father and sister means yet. With Kobe and Gianna went, and Bianka and Capri being the youngest members of the family, we believe Vanessa and Natalia to be the rocks of their family in carrying out their Kobe's legacy in terms of sports, love, and devotion.

We knew about Kobe Bryant merely as a successful basketball player, just another celebrity in the world of sports. But his tragic death inspired us to dig in his life to know better. Little did we know about the love he carried for his lifelines which were his captivating wife and the daughters. Kobe's love for them was unfathomable and losing them was something Vanessa never guessed.

The father-daughter duo was buried in Pacific View Memorial Park in the Corona del Mar neighborhood of Newport Beach, California on February 7. It was a private ceremony which was attended by very close family and friends and involved quite a turmoil of emotions. It was cathartic and a moment from their lives which they did not want to share with the outside world. Later a memorial service was held on February 24 at the Staples Center in Downtown Los Angeles where the family and several renowned celebrities paid their tributes to the deceased Bryants. The public memorial for Kobe and Gigi was titled "Celebration of Life for Kobe and Gianna Bryant".

At the service, Vanessa said in her speech about her late husband and baby daughter: She was overwhelmed when she pointed out the fact that God knew they were inseparable when they were alive in this world. That is why God has decided to call both them together to Him-self. She addressed directly to Kobe saying to take care of their daughter, Gianna. At some point in her speech, she was telling the audience what kind of a family person Kobe was. Even after a very intense match, he would make an effort to put his family first and how he was sincere towards his priorities. Amidst all these powerful celebrity performances and their tributes during the memorial service, Vanessa and Natalia stood at the podium and shared tiny aspects of their lives. This gave the world an insight into how humble they all were and how simple was their approach towards life.

We have always been a fan of the LA Lakers legend and his loving family and the grief they are dealing with at the moment is very sudden and the news was so unexpected we believe the world was not ready to take in. At this point in time, whenever we sit to discuss or even think of Vanessa Bryant and the kids, we can feel nothing but empathy as to what tragedy they have stumbled upon. We cannot go by talking about them now without reference to that horrific helicopter crash, or Gianna, who was also an upcoming legend in the world of basketball or Kobe Bryant, the legend himself.

Life has come to a halt for Kobe's Queen Mamba. But she is swift enough to recover and stay strong for her girls who need her now more than ever. We all know grieving and mourning are part of the healing process, the world needs to give the Bryant family that precious phase to re-visit those special and mundane moments of their lives. Amidst all these talks about grieving, mourning, and pain, the Bryant's are staying strong for the fans. Vanessa Bryant is active on Instagram and has recently posted an image of Natalia Bryant posing in front of a mural.

The mural is of Kobe kissing her baby Gigi on the forehead. Kobe's queen mamba posted another photo of herself with her three daughters in front of the giant mural, captioned with lyrics from the song "Smile" by Nat King Cole. We hope they keep smiling the way they were on the photos; after all, it takes courage to get back to smiling and be the epitome of moral support for so many people. Our prayers are with the Bryant's in all spheres of their lives. Rest in peace the souls of Kobe and Gigi and may God bless the Bryant's in good spirit and health.

His Food Choices

Kobe looked in shape and fit in all his NBA games but have you ever wondered what goes behind making this body of steel? Do you think it is all work-out and gyms? It takes a lot of guts to stay away from the food you love and see in front of you all the time. Kobe loved food and he was accustomed to eating meat, fast food, junks, and sugar. For him, it became a part of his life to eat like a regular person but after reaching a certain age, metabolism starts to become weak. The lifestyle you are habituated with for a long time needs improvement. Kobe also faced that problem where he was not feeling as active as he was before due to his food choice.

With the help of his trainer, Kobe did hardcore exercise, crucial training every day in the gym or in the basketball court. Along with that Kobe had to cut down on his favorite type of foods. No matter how hard he trained, an imbalanced diet was ruining his body and his stamina. He had to give up red meat and added more vegetables and fruits in his diet. He was not a fan of consuming pro-biotic as some of them carry major side effects in the long run. He omitted junk food or fast food from his diet. It was a difficult choice to make for Kobe. He was accustomed to this type of food for a long time. But he knew in his head, to be fit and better than before, he needs to make wise food choices. He cannot give in to his cravings.

He explained in many interviews that his fight against fast food and red meat is difficult but he made a conscious decision of avoiding those. Playing well and being fit was more important than delighting his taste buds. It is not like healthy food tastes bad. If you have a good chef, they can swift up something delicious even out of the healthiest ingredients.

Kobe trained for a long time in a day so he lost a lot of his strength and stamina after a workout. To replenish nutrition back in the body Kobe's diet was balanced by certified nutrition. For proteins, he ate chicken, cheese, Greek yogurt, and beans. He had carbohydrates like oats and quinoa in his diet. He had lots of fresh fruits in his diet. To detoxify his body, he used to drink green tea without sugar. It also relaxes the body quite well. Staying hydrated is essential for everyone and when you work so hard every single day, you need proper water to sustain.

He also had a lot of fresh veggies in his diet. He did not eat red meat per se, but he ate the liver and liverwurst. Rotisserie chicken was one of his favorite dishes. Ezekiel Bread was another personal favorite for Kobe. Fermented food is good for the body so Kobe ate sauerkraut quite often. He also ate sprouts in his salads. His diet involved a lot of salads as he has to work-out for a long time he had to eat 5-6 servings of salad throughout the day.

Kobe's Workout

As an NBA player, Kobe had to go the extra mile when it comes to fitness. His work did not allow him to slow down unless there is an injury in the body. Kobe had a reputation for playing with injuries in the past. But the coach, the trainer never supported this act of Kobe. To stay in the best form Kobe did the 666 work-out with his trainer. He did this work-out only during his NBA off-seasons. The weird name is given due to working out for 6 months a year, 6 days a week and 6 hours a day. This is no joke, 6 hours out of 24 hours devoted to only working out is a hard job. Someone who is very determined can achieve this. Kobe did it effortlessly.

Kobe did not make it monotonous. His 6 hours or working out was divided into one hour of cardio. Two hours of basketball skills, two hours of track work and one hour of weight lifting. All of these exercises contributed to making Kobe a fit and active athlete.

The track work Kobe did include High-intensity interval training. It meant basically to sprint or jog or walk for about 100-400 yards. This is pretty hardcore for an average person to achieve.

Kobe did both Olympic style weight lifting and the traditional weight lifting. Traditional weight lifting builds your muscles and increases your stamina. Olympic weight lifting focuses on high verticals and explosive movements.

A large number of hours he spent in his basketball drills. Kobe shoot about 700-1000 shot on a daily basis. An average person would be tired after the first 100. But Kobe was always determined. Kobe also did 20 minutes of basketball dribbling every day. Kobe practiced defensive slides for 10 minutes daily. Then he did 90 minutes of intense shoot-around. He pointed out five different areas in the basketball court and practiced shooting from those areas for 10 times each. Then he did mid-range shoots and followed by a three-point line shooting. He did practice turn-around shots, pivots jobs and post-up shots too. In the very end, he practiced footwork and layups.

All of these exercises make him a strong basketball player in the court. He was not born with all those skills, rather he had to work hard to develop these skills. Kobe was always focused on developing skills and he knew by pushing hard anyone can achieve greatness.

Kobe's off-season workout was insane in itself but his in-season workout is unbelievable. He increased the condition of his workout as the season nears. It will drive an average person crazy if they ever had to follow what Kobe goes through. The only reason he rested for one day of the week was to give rest to his body and muscles. He wanted to reach muscle hypertrophy and to achieve that he performed 8-12 reps.

His days were assigned by his trainer to work on certain aspects of the body so that they can always stay fit and active.

Kobe Bryant And His "Mamba Mentality"

My heart is heavy on the sudden demise of the great basketball player and a man of iron personality Kobe Bryant. As a tribute to him, I would like to share thoughts and lessons from his life summarized in the topic 'Kobe Bryant's Mamba Mentality'.

The nickname Black Mamba was given to Kobe by himself. Its origin was from the sexual assault case on him that left all the sponsors except Nike to drop him out. Each person was telling him that he just can't do it again. It is very easy to assume the difficult time he was passing through. But the obstacle couldn't stop him. This actually made him stronger enough to attack the opposition like a Mamba. He responded by a public apology as part of the settlement, but later all charges were dropped. He took an initiative to rebrand his image. But he was thinking about how to do this. He was inspired by the mamba snake in the movie Quentin Tarantino's *Kill Bill*. A lethal mamba snake was there as an assassin. Since then he was popularly known as Black Mamba.

People often say that Mamba mentality was a basketball centered thought of Kobe. But the reality is it is something more than that. It is a firm search to know the unknown. It is the process of getting better each day. It inspires you to go forward for the highest level of achievement not being worried about the real outcome. When we take initiative to become successful the greatest enemy to us is our thoughts that "what others will say". The Black Mamba says, "Don't really worry about others' thoughts, their disappointments, and just focus on your present and your performance".

In an Amazon book review, Kobe himself explained Mamba Mentality as "Focusing on the process and keep firm belief in hard work when it matters". It's the ultimate key for a competitive spirit. Kobe used to start the workout at 4 a.m. and tried to do more than his competitors. He believed in hard work and practice but always left the outcome on luck. Bryant had a personality and success history that made some people love him and some got jealous. It was easy for the mass people to conclude that Kobe's talents are god gifted. But the truth is all the people with God gifted talents are not successful like Kobe. The hard work and dedication he had given for making the path perfect distinguish him from others.

Kobe made his sincerest 20-year career on the base of firm self-confidence. Confidence and dedication are words closely attached to his personality. If any fellow wants to lead a life like him he has to be impassioned and committed with zero worries.

When Kobe went to his retirement from his long basketball carrier, he decided to enlighten other hearts by writing a book and letting people know his lifelong learning. There are lots of fresh players, his fans and students of basketball who were the target readers of his book. He named his book-'Mamba Mentality", based on the lifelong struggle and hard work he passed through to become such a nonpareil player.

Charity Work Of Kobe

If you look at Kobe's life, you will notice the remarkable effort he has given in terms of building opportunities for others. It did not matter to him that he was a legendary NBA player when it came to doing deeds for others. He was never content with his comfortable mansion, his private helicopter or his $2 billion worth business. He always got pleasure by creating opportunities for others and helping others.

Since he is into sports passionately, his area of charity started from people who also have a love for sports. He always wanted to help underprivileged kids. Before his death, he was working on a children's book that was supposed to help the underprivileged kids. It is a shame that the world could not see this masterpiece and people could not benefit from it.

Kobe was ASAS's official ambassador. It is After School All-star association which is an American non-profit organization. This organization gave special after school pieces of training to children in 13 different cities in the USA. Kobe had a special link with China and China had a huge fan following Kobe in there. Kobe took full advantage of that popularity and built a Kobe Bryant China Fund. This fundraising program was in partnership with the Soong Ching Ling Foundation. It was no ordinary foundations; it was backed up by the Chinese Government. So it could reach any area of China and spread the light. The fund raised money chiefly for their health and education. These are the two main focuses of it and if they become interested in sports, it also enlightened them with knowledge.

Another good charity work of Kobe was for the Call of Duty Endowment. On November 4, 2010, in the launch of *Call of Duty: Black Ops, Kobe donated a $1* million check to the non-profit organization. The organization was responsible for creating civil jobs for retired military service holders. This is a great way to use the skills of those veterans and give them another opportunity for another job. It also helped them to motivate them to live an active life. Military life is a routine and busy life. When you retire, suddenly everything stops and you get into a depression. For most people, depression is a must after retirement and this organization helped those to try fresh and a new career. Kobe found the cause very interesting and helpful and that motivated him to donate a handsome number. The event was at the Santa Monica Airport and Kobe appeared with Zach Braff there.

KVBFF (Kobe and Vanessa Bryant Family Foundation was another successful charity work of Kobe. They focused on young people again in this foundation. Kobe in his investments and in his social works, always prioritized youth because he knew with a little bit of motivation and training they can become big. He knew every individual has something they can offer to humanity and it needs development. He offered development in this foundation. They also focused on homeless people with this foundation. They targeted these young people and tried to train them to improve their skills and make them interested in different sports. Kobe was a basketball player but he never stuck to his own game when he was preaching the positivity of sports in life. He encouraged all forms of sports and he knew whoever feels passionate about a sport, they should be given the chance and proper training to improve it further.

Bryant always wanted to do good for the people to the best of his ability. Becoming a great basketball player has always been a dream but he was never content of being Known as a great basketball player. He wanted to leave a mark in people's hearts, which led him to constantly search for people in need. Kobe also took special care for homeless people. According to Kobe, homeless people are not trash. They have potential, it is not their own fault that they ended up being jobless and homeless. We need to give them a chance too and see if they can do something productive. So his foundation tried hard to improve the condition of the homeless.

When someone is deemed as useless, they tend to sit around and be lazy as opposed to trying to find out their hidden potential. Similarly, when someone motivates another, they try and find out their skills and then develop it further. In short, Kobe knew the power of positive thinking and believing in people. Homelessness cannot be someone's weakness and Kobe knew it well. He wanted the entire world to accept that a large part of the society in any country is homeless and we cannot stop caring for them because of their poverty. They also need basic things to survive. This shows how much of a big-hearted person he was.

Another big charity work of his life was for the National Museum of African American History and Culture. He was a founding donor for this foundation. It was located in Washington DC. It was founded in 2003 and it became permanent in 2016. This donation of his proves he is proud of his roots and he wanted to give back to the community where he came from originally.

Kobe's contribution to the "Make-A-Wish" foundation is remarkable as well. This foundation brings wishes alive from children to teens that are ill or suffering from poverty.

They aged between 2.5 years to 18 years. In his entire lifetime, Kobe made about 200 wishes come true. Can you believe it? This means granting wishes from 200 different kids. Kobe had three kids who were very fortunate that they were healthy and wealthy. Kobe acknowledged that poverty and illness can be very devastating for any kid. When you do small acts of kindness for the kids, the smile you see in their faces is what encouraged Kobe to be affiliated with this foundation. It was not only the kids who felt the joy after their wishes came true, but Kobe was also equally happy when each of their wishes could come true because of him.

The Tragic End

It was just another day of my life. Like every other day I got back home after a long day of work, I sat with a mug of hot coffee and my mobile, I came across the news of Kobe Bryant and his beloved daughter, Gianna Maria-Onore Bryant's tragic death. I kept on scrolling up and down the newsfeed only trying to gather all sorts of news blurbs to know the details of what happened, how it happened and when it happened. The news not only broke my heart but was among one of the top headlines of 2020 to date which shook the world to a great extent.

Did I know the Bryant family personally? No, I did not. But going through (almost) all the news coverage and short clips of the family's sneak peek into their intimate moments enthused me to get to know them better and feel the passion of the basketball game and get to know-how a celebrity family enjoys time with their loved ones and also read up about how the family of a late legend mourns.

Kobe was only 41 years old when he met a tragic end to his life. No one deemed this NBA legend would go away like this. People were still in shock even after the dead bodies were recognized as his. They could not believe and they did not want to believe that he is gone forever. When you love and follow someone for a long time, you only wish good things for them. You want them to be happy and productive all their lives. A tragic end like a helicopter crash is not something anyone would imagine as a good ending.

In January 2020, Kobe humped on his helicopter with the pilot. It was a Sikorsky S-76 helicopter. They departed from Orange country, California from the John Wayne airport. It was not Kobe alone, in the helicopter he had six of his family friends and his daughter Gianna with him. She was only 13 years old. The helicopter registered Fillmore-based Island Express Holding Corp. They were headed to Thousand Oaks to attend a Mamba Family's basketball game. They wanted to land in Ventura County at Camarillo Airport.

It was not a good day to fly in that morning. The sky was slightly foggy and it was lightly rainy that morning. For light rain and fog, most air traffic and LA police dept helicopter decided not to fly. They grounded most of the flights for that morning. Kobe's helicopter was circling above the LA zoo for quite some time. It was facing heavy air traffic at that moment. The pilot sent a signal to the Burbank Airport's control tower. The pilot notified the control tower about his situation. The control tower replied that the pilot was flying too low. It was too low that they could not track the helicopter by radar. At that time, it was about 9.30 am. The pilot saw heavy fog and could not make his vision clear. During 9.40 am, the pilot decided to move towards the south towards the mountains. The pilot made a drastic move by climbing from 1200 feet to 2000 feet above. It was flying at 161 knots.

At 9.45 am the helicopter crashed. In Calabasas, it hit a side of the mountain. It was 30 miles away from downtown LA. The helicopter began to burn after the crash. Everyone, Kobe, Gianna, the Pilot and the six family friends were killed instantly. The witnessed from far saw the helicopter struggling in heavy fog moments before it finally crashed in flames.

Since Kobe was a legend and a renowned celebrity, proper investigations followed through with his death. The actual reason behind his helicopter crash did not come out. The helicopter was for Kobe's personal use, so he never added a black box to it. Three renowned institutes like the FBI, FAA and National Transportation Safety Board made their investigations on Kobe's helicopter crash separately. Since it was a helicopter crash and its brunt after the crash, it was difficult to identify the people in it.

Kobe's body got recognized with his fingerprints on January 28, 2 days after the helicopter crash. In these two days, his family and fans hopes for a miracle and they thought they would not have to hear the horrible news. But no one can deny the truth and they had to make peace with the departure of their favorite icon. All the nine people in the helicopter died of blunt force trauma due to the crash of the helicopter. Afterward, they were burnt. This information was provided by the Los Angeles County Department of Medical Examiner-Coroner.

The bodies of Kobe and his daughter Gianna were finally buried in California on February 7. It was in Newport Beach, in the Corona del Mar neighborhood. It was a private burial ceremony in Pacific View Memorial Park. Only the friend, and family of Kobe attended the event. They decided not to mark their graves to protect their privacy.

Since he was a legend, they thought it would be risky to engrave their titles on their graves.

The public memorial service happened on February 24. It was in downtown LA at the Staples Center. It was the Laker's hometown where Kobe had so much history.

Conclusion

Kobe was a giant in NBA history with so many records and skills. In his 20 years of NBA career, he had both ups and downs where he had to come to terms with retiring early for his numerous injuries from time to time. The time when he was best at his game, he always remembered where he came from. He never abandoned his roots and always respected it. People may point finger at few misfortunes of Kobe's life but when you look at the bigger picture, you will see only a few hurdles but a lot of successes.

He not only became an NBA legend but tried different things too. He tried his luck in music because he had a profound love for music since he was in school. With many attempts when music was not favoring him properly, he decided to tell stories. He always wanted to be creative and tell stories. His love for the NBA was unconditional but after his retirement, his love for story-telling was no less. He felt very passionately for the idea of telling different stories to inspire people, particularly the youth.

The vision he had to improve the society around him, particularly in terms of sports deserved to applaud. He was not content in one thing alone, he tried many things and invested in many sectors. His vision was to expand the potential of people who cannot support themselves. He had a keen eye for talents. He was most successful when he invested in startups built by unknown people. He had a strong belief in the power of positivity. When Kobe sat with someone for a project if the vibe was good he did not wait to sign him up. He did not care about his homelessness or his insufficient budget. He always cared for the unfortunate people and the underprivileged kids.

In 19 years long marriage, Kobe had one hurdle and the rest went pretty smooth. In 2003, the adulterous encounter was the only time Kobe was unfaithful to his wife. They both solved the problem with grace and they took the bigger picture in their priority. They decided to work on their marriage one more time and it did run smoothly afterward. They had four beautiful kids together and the marriage stood strong for all those years.

The person whom we have watched running within the basketball court is also a family man. Family is the place from where he has got his strength to move forward. All the encouragement and inspiration which he got from his parents are transmitted later to his daughter. He has proven himself to be a great father. His wife has become the right companion throughout their life journey. So, besides being a famous player outside, he is also an affectionate human being with his family. From his very childhood day, the love for basketball grew into him and as a result, he is known today before the whole world as KOBE BRYANT.

His numerous endeavors with different charity foundations and his own charity foundation show how caring as a human being he was. He wanted to do a lot more, he wanted to tell a lot of stories in inspiration. He could not fulfill all his dreams but the limited gems that he left behind are enough to make him unforgettable for the people.

Printed in Great Britain
by Amazon